POWER
TO
PERSUADE

HOW TO LEAD PEOPLE

TO TRANSFORMATIONAL DECISIONS

May you experience unprecedented success this year!

Summit Books, LLC.
© 2014 by Jason Frenn
All rights reserved.

ISBN 978-0-9913881-4-1

All scripture quotations are from THE HOLY BIBLE, NEW INTERNATIONAL VERSION®, NIV® Copyright © 1973, 1978, 1984, 2011 by Bíblica, Inc.® Used by permission. All rights reserved worldwide.

Cover design Rick Cortez

Cover photo Jazmin Frenn

Printed in the United States of America
First Edition: October 2014

Also by Jason Frenn

Power To Change
Breaking the Barriers
Power To Reinvent Yourself
The Seven Prayers God Always Answers
Become What You Believe

Available wherever books are sold.
Visit www.JasonFrenn.com

Dedicated to

*Two of the finest examples of
generous philanthropy,
Christian character,
compassionate dedication,
unwavering commitment*

Don and Maxine Judkins

POWER TO PERSUADE

HOW TO LEAD PEOPLE

TO TRANSFORMATIONAL DECISIONS

JASON FRENN

Summit Books, LLC
Jackson, Wyoming

Contents

Introduction   1

Section I   Persuasive Leadership

Chapter 1   Become Someone People Want to Follow   9
Chapter 2   Visualize Where People Need to Go   26

Section II   Persuasive Communication

Chapter 3   Become a Powerful Communicator   51
Chapter 4   How to Communicate Powerfully   76

Section III Persuasive Solutions

Chapter 5   Breaking Your Glass Ceiling   98
Chapter 6   Overcoming Obstacles, Objections, and
              Rejections   119

Section IV Persuasive Closing

Chapter 7   Become a Powerful Closer   141
Chapter 8   The Ten Most Powerful Closes   161

Conclusion   185
Endnotes   191
Acknowledgements   193

INTRODUCTION

In 1988, I walked into the interview for my first job after graduating from college. The company that interviewed me was Moore Business Forms, a multinational corporation that sold printed materials to businesses. On the one hand, I was excited about starting a career where I would be pulling in a salary. On the other hand, I didn't even know what a business form was. I had a vague idea of what an invoice looked like, so I had a point of reference of sorts. Still, how could I get excited about that? What meaning could I find in selling paper to businesses? I needed a job, though. So I continued the interview process, although I would have to come to grips with that nagging question about meaningful work.

Finding Significance

In my final interview, the regional manager of western sales asked me a question that helped me see things from a different perspective. He asked, "If we were at your retirement dinner in forty years and all your colleagues stood up and said something about you, what would you want them to say?" No one had ever asked me that question before.

I immediately responded, "That's a great question. Give me a moment to ponder it." After a few seconds I said, "I would want them to say that I was a man of integrity, someone who helped others, and did what I said I would do."

He looked at me without blinking, waited several seconds, then grinned ever so slightly and said, "Can you begin on the first of the month?" He hired me because he saw that two of my core values were integrity and commitment.

Introduction

I started the job the following month. After three days of sales training, I faced that question of how to find meaning in selling paper to businesses. *Of course, I'll make money*, I thought. But life isn't just about making money. Life is about meaning, significance, and finding what I call your *golden thread*.

Too many people stumble through life without a clue of what is their golden thread. Your golden thread is what you were born to do. It's who you were wired to be. Your gifts, talents, and abilities indicate patterns of direction, and they will guide you to become excellent in a given area.

I felt that my golden thread was to persuade people and help them live better lives. That's when a spark ignited a flame to help me through those years when I sold paper to businesses. You see I sold invoices, payroll checks, insurance forms, and letterhead. These different types of forms weren't just paper with ink on them. The sale of a business form provided funds to hundreds of thousands of people. When I sold ten thousand payroll checks to Oakley, a maker of sporting sunglasses, for example, the people who worked in the Moore Business manufacturing plant worked hard to print the material. Those employees received a salary and paid their bills. In addition, the company who serviced the printing presses performed maintenance, and eventually the press manufacturer received orders for new presses. The paper mill produced the paper. Drivers drove the tree trunks to the mills to convert the wood into paper. And yes, loggers had to cut the trees. Everyone throughout the process received compensation as a result of that payroll check order. In addition, those who worked at Oakley received their salary on the checks that we designed. The checks were deposited into their bank accounts so they could pay their bills and put food on the table for their families. I found meaning and significance in selling paper to businesses, and I used my golden thread to do it effectively.

If I could somehow find significance in selling paper, I have little doubt that you can find significance in the work you were made to do. I believe that when you discover your golden thread, you will become highly effective and successful in ways that you have yet to imagine. If that is one of your desires, read on. I am about to share with you what is at the heart of this book.

The Skill of Persuasion

In every attempted transaction there is a seller and a buyer. Either the seller persuades the buyer that she should buy, or the buyer convinces the seller that she shouldn't buy. Whether it's a product, service, philosophy, or idea, people buy something or reject it depending upon how persuasive the presentation is. Whether you are the president of a major corporation, an entrepreneur, manager, housewife, or student, someone will try to convince you to do something every day of your life. And the greatest achievers will be those with the ability to persuade you and others.

Regardless of your line of work, your ability to persuade directly determines how far you will go and how fast you'll get there. It determines how much money you will make and how many lives you will impact. Your ability to persuade will help you carve out the life you dream of having and help you maintain it. Your ability to persuade will impact nearly every area of your life, including your spouse, children, and the legacy you leave behind. Why? Because persuasion is simply the art of getting people to follow you. The people you persuade will

Introduction

follow your advice to buy something. They will follow your lead when they feel lost. They will look to you for marriage counsel. They will follow you on social media and even read your books. If you are persuasive enough, they will follow you to the ends of the earth.

The book you hold in your hands will show you powerful life-changing tools. It will show you how to lead people to a point of making decisions that can alter their lives for the better. In essence, these tools help you guide people as they make transformational decisions. If you implement the principles we discuss in the following chapters, you will become much more persuasive, powerful, affluent, and ultimately more successful. The content of this book will empower you to reach your goals with greater efficiency and swiftness.

The concepts we'll discuss in this book are powerful, but if they are implemented inappropriately the result could be damaging. That is why integrity is one of the anchors of the *power to persuade*. Without integrity, we become self-centered, apathetic, irrelevant, and ultimately destructive. With integrity, we ensure that we are heading in the right direction and that we aim for what is best for everyone we seek to serve.

Do you consider yourself highly successful or slightly above average? Are you reaching your greatest potential or are you caught in a holding pattern? Are you where you want to be? Are you doing what you want to do? If not, perhaps what holds you back is your ability to persuade. My goal in this book is to help you become a persuasive *leader*, a persuasive *communicator*, a persuasive *problem solver*, and a persuasive *closer*. Each one of these four areas is pertinent to having a great career, business, family, and marriage.

Our Road Map

The first step in our journey is the most important. It is this: unless *you* are persuaded, you will never be able to persuade others. Before you can sell, you have to first buy. I tell salespeople that they need to own their own products when feasible. They must believe that their product is the greatest in the world. If they don't, they need to work for the company that produces the greatest products. The same is true for leaders. They must believe that their organization is the finest and that the people they lead are the best. If not, they should work to make it the best. Regardless of your line of work, the company for which you work, your career, or position, be persuaded. Take this book and its contents seriously. Don't underestimate the power to persuade and the important role it plays in each of the four areas mentioned above—leadership, communication, solution, and closing. If you truly want to reach your greatest potential and move beyond what holds you back, you need to embrace the power to persuade.

As I have indicated, *Power to Persuade* is divided into four sections—persuasive leadership, persuasive communication, persuasive problem solving, and persuasive closing. First, we will look at how persuasive leaders build healthy morale and how that permeates the entire organization. You'll learn the best way to discover what you were wired to do and to help others discover their golden thread.

Second, you'll learn what makes people great persuasive communicators in their speaking, writing, and leading. Persuasive communication is one of the powerful ways to lead people and guide them to transformational decisions.

In the third section, you'll learn how to become a persuasive

Introduction

problem solver so that everyone involved will benefit. Your negotiation skills will increase as well as your ability to gain the confidence of others.

Finally, you'll learn some of the best ways to bring closure to transactions, agreements, and sales opportunities, as well as to some of the most important decisions of your life. Many people know how to lead. Few can lead *and* communicate. Fewer can lead, communicate, and problem solve, and even fewer adequately implement all four. My hope is that by the end of this book you will have learned to master all of these skills.

Let me add that I come from what I humorously call a crazy family. My mom and dad were separated when I was three, divorced when I was nine, and married other people. Between all my parents there are eleven divorces. My mom was my stepfather's sixth wife. As you can imagine, family reunions were interesting.

All this family turmoil took its toll on me. My study habits were horrible. I watched my fellow classmates excel while I struggled to understand the material. I was a terrible reader and none of my written essays made any sense. None of my teachers thought that I would grow up to be an author and conference speaker. So how did I?

Obviously, something happened to change my course. You'll pick up some of the clues throughout the pages of this book, but I will give you the explicit answer in the conclusion. Please don't skip ahead. It's important that you make this journey as it was intended. I mention this so that you will know that if I can make it, so can you. If you are facing incredible adversity, I believe you can overcome. Just be faithful to read this book cover to cover and put into practice what it says.

As we bring the introduction to a close, I want to encourage you. You didn't pick up this book by chance. You are not reading it by accident. You have a purpose in life. You have a great destiny. You have a wonderfully bright future. So begin to visualize the potential you have to become all you're destined to be. I believe this book will play a huge part in your reaching your greatest potential. If you're serious about gaining the power to persuade and lead others to transformational decisions, turn the page, and let's begin that journey together.

Section I

Persuasive Leadership

Chapter 1

BECOME SOMEONE PEOPLE WANT TO FOLLOW

You are both a leader and a follower. The people you're with at the moment determine which one you are. My question is when you are a leader are you a good one? You can be an effective leader without being a boss, but you can't be an effective boss without being an effective leader. So what characterizes an effective leader? They know where they are going. They genuinely believe in the mission while keeping their followers' best interests in mind. In short, a leader is someone people want to follow.

How do you become someone people want to follow? In this chapter, we'll look at the values that every persuasive leader has and how those values set him or her apart from mediocre leaders. By reading this chapter, you'll learn how to create healthy morale around you and how to positively impact your entire organization. Let's take a look at the first trait found in great leaders—*integrity*.

1. Integrity

David moved to the United States from Mexico when he was six years old. After sixty-five years of peaceful living in San Diego, he received a letter from the IRS stating that they wanted to see the books of his businesses going back three years. He cautiously agreed. As the representative analyzed David's financial transactions, something uncommon stood out. David had reportedly given away millions of dollars to charitable organizations. The IRS representative became highly suspicious.

He said, "You supposedly gave away close to $5 million over the past three years, and I find that hard to believe. We're going to continue this investigation going back seven years. We need to see all the receipts for your charitable contributions over the period we're investigating." David instructed his accountant to provide what the IRS agent wanted.

The accountant scoured storage facilities and filing cabinets until every receipt and cancelled check was found. Three weeks passed, and finally the agent rendered a decision. At first, he found it difficult to believe that someone would start and maintain several businesses for the sole purpose of supporting his favorite non-profit organizations. After thoroughly investigating each transaction, the IRS agent found a flawless accounting system backed by a man of high integrity. The representative decided to write David a letter congratulating him on his record keeping and philanthropy. David can go where he wants to go, do what he wants to do, and buy whatever he wants to buy. When I asked him what his most valuable trait was, he replied, "My integrity is the foundation upon which I built all my successes." This is one of the reasons people throughout his organization highly value his example. Persuasive leaders have integrity and live their lives beyond reproach even when it seems no one is watching.

Whether you are a CEO, housewife, small business owner, doctor, teacher, single parent, athlete, factory worker, or student, the most important leadership quality you can have is integrity. You can't buy it. You can't borrow it. If you lose it, it's difficult to regain. It's the foundation for every other leadership trait. It's the standard for doing the right thing when no one is there to stop you or congratulate you. If you want people to follow you, you must demonstrate a commitment to live beyond reproach. You may not be responsible for the name your parents gave you, but you are responsible for what people think when they hear your name. So when people think about you, they should think of someone honest and upright. They should think that you are a person of your word and that your standards are decent and good. In their minds, you do not lie nor do you tolerate it. You do not cheat and will not collaborate with those who do. You do not talk out of both sides of your mouth. Persuasive leaders are not wishy-washy. They attract people who trust them, and nothing builds trust quicker than integrity.

2. Dedication

On March 13, 1996, I had high expectations and much enthusiasm for an event I had organized. There was only one problem. I was the only one excited about the event. One month before, I had purchased a forty-foot flatbed trailer, a sound system, stage lighting, and a 13,000-watt generator. I organized a tour to travel from town to town holding open-air meetings to help gang members, drug addicts, and people living in marginalized areas. I had a desire since college to help underprivileged young people break free from their destructive patterns.

The first night of the meeting two friends and I arrived early to set up all the gear. I contracted a musical group to open the show, but none of them arrived until it was time for their performance. None of my family members came at all. I worked all day, jumped into the back of my minivan, shaved, put on a sports coat, and hosted the event.

Become Someone People Want to Follow

Despite a lack of support from those close to me, something wonderful developed. By the third event, the crowds numbered over fifteen hundred. That's when my family and friends began to see my strong commitment and eventually came alongside to help.

Do people hesitate to follow you? If so, they may need assurance that you are committed to doing what you said you would do. If they care about your cause and feel that it's worthy, they'll look for a reason to trust you. But don't expect people to rally around you at the beginning. Donors wait, coordinators are reluctant, workers are slow, and volunteers hold off until they are convinced you are dedicated. That assurance always takes time.

As I look back, I clearly see that in the beginning I didn't provide the assurance people needed to trust me. When I started, I had no track record. Twenty-five years later, though, I've spoken to over four million people in live events around the world, some of them secular, some of them religious. Today, it's much easier to acquire the support, backing, and volunteers needed, because there is a record of dedication and consistency.

It's difficult to lead others when you are not fully dedicated to the cause. When a leader is conflicted, people detect it. Followers can only be as dedicated to the cause as their leader is. That's one major problem with politics today. Few people believe that politicians are unconditionally dedicated to what they proclaim. The general sentiment around the world is that politicians shield the truth, withhold information, and simply tell their constituents what they want to hear. When people doubt a leader's dedication, they won't follow that leader. So if you want to be a persuasive leader, be clearly and genuinely dedicated to your cause.

Power To Persuade

As people observe you, they size you up. Sooner or later, your actions will paint an accurate picture of your convictions and what's important to you. People may or may not believe what you say, but they will believe what you do. Actions *do* speak louder than words. Your actions show others how committed you are to the vision. Leaders who make self-sacrificing choices for the mission demonstrate their dedication and thus build a strong following.

Today, I heard a news report about an individual who has worked for a New Hampshire cab company for thirty-six years. After starting out answering the phones, the person moved up to become a cab driver and has done so for the last twenty-six years, working from nine to five, Monday through Friday. The driver never uses a GPS, never calls in sick, always drives the speed limit, and is one of the most requested workers in the fleet. She is turning ninety years old, and has helped many in her organization by setting a great example of dedication and consistency. I've met many cab drivers in my lifetime, but few have those credentials and consistency. Aunt Dottie's dedication to hard work is obvious. It points to a strong work ethic that people find attractive.[1] If I were lost on the East Coast, I would trust someone like Aunt Dottie to point me in the right direction. For nearly four decades, her actions have spoken louder than words. Followers are in search of leaders whose actions are consistent with their words. Show your dedication and people will follow.

3. Wisdom

I sat across the table from one of the greatest communicators in Latin America. He had a four-minute daily program that aired on television stations throughout the continent. The audio feed from his television program went to hundreds of radio stations that aired the same day. The transcript of the audio went to newspapers in nearly twenty countries for his daily column. Each day, over 1,100 television and radio stations and newspapers transmitted his thought for the day. I asked him over breakfast, "What's one of the most important lessons you've learned over the years?"

Without hesitating he said, "I try not to surround myself with people who are simply intelligent. Smart people can be arrogant. Instead, I surround myself with wise people. You cannot be wise and arrogant, because with wisdom comes humility."

It's been nearly twenty years since we had that conversation, and I can say beyond any doubt that he was absolutely right. Wise leaders make sound decisions, and when they don't, they are the first to admit their mistake.

Some leaders are dedicated and have integrity, but finding one that embraces wisdom as well is rare. Wisdom sets great leaders apart from the rest of the pack. They listen before they speak. They render their decisions and form their opinions with caution. As they decide where to move, when to change jobs, where to study, or who to marry, persuasive leaders use wise deliberation, which shows their followers their consideration of the different options.

When people describe you, do they use the word *wise*? Do they come to you for advice? Do they call you and say, "I need your input." In a meeting do they say, "I'd like to hear your opinion on the matter"? If not, now is the time to become someone people want to follow, someone people look to for wisdom.

Power To Persuade

If you want to be effective at persuading people to make transformational decisions, you must convey that you hear them. They need to sense that you've taken the time to intentionally consider the different outcomes of every possible decision that affect them and that you care. When your followers feel that your decisions are guided by discernment and sound judgment, their confidence in you will increase. As you demonstrate the ability to accurately forecast a prudent and healthy outcome for them, your circle of trusted followers will solidify and grow.

Wisdom cannot be measured, but it's a skill that can be developed. And since it is a skill, it can be learned and taught. One question that I often am asked is how can a person become wiser? If you live out the three following principles you will gain wisdom that you can apply in every area of your life.

First, *spend time with people who are wise*. Watch how they make decisions. Discover their paradigm for life. A wise man once wrote, "Do not be misled: 'Bad company corrupts good character'" (1 Corinthians 15:33). An ancient king once said, "He who walks with the wise grows wise, but a companion of fools suffers harm" (Proverbs 13:20). You've heard the old adage "birds of a feather flock together." You will tend to become like the six people with whom you spend the most time (your children and family count as one).

Second, *when faced with a decision, ask yourself if you are* reacting *or* responding. A reaction can be defensive. It can be explosive and serve as a backlash. A response, on the other hand, is planned and thoughtful. It can serve as a healthy way to resolve conflict or render a decision. This is true in your family, marriage, and friendships. It's true with your boss, children, employees, clients, and management team. Learn to respond and not overreact. Weigh the consequences of your words

15

before you open your mouth.

Third, *read literature filled with wisdom that provokes thought*. Then allow those words to sink in and help form your thought processes when you're faced with an important decision. The Bible book of Proverbs is a great place to begin. While wisdom is perhaps one of the greatest attributes of a leader, it is not the final one. Leaders who are persuasive must also be honorable and aligned with honorable causes.

4. Honor

Maria was a single mother who lived on the streets of Central America. She sold her body for money to feed her two small children. She and her girls slept under a plastic tarp that was fastened to two wooden crates. A friend of mine who lives in Latin America walked by her makeshift home and decided to intervene. He told Maria, "I want to put a real roof over your head." At first, she thought that he was lying or wanted something significant in return. He assured her that she wouldn't owe him a cent. He contacted some donors, found a small lot, and arranged to build her and her two daughters a new home. It wasn't a mansion by any means, but the 525 square foot cement block home gave her the one thing every human being wants—dignity. Once the home was complete, his organization offered her classes so that she could learn an employable trade.

After two years, Maria's life was revolutionized. She had a job that allowed her to provide for her family's needs. She was the proud owner of a small one-bedroom house with a bathroom and indoor plumbing. Afterward, my friend showed his donors what he had done with their finances and simply said, "There's another Maria living somewhere on the streets of this Central American city. Please help me find her. I want to help her get back on her feet." Over the past several years, my friend has helped hundreds of single mothers like Maria find a way out of misery.

Clearly, not everyone works on the streets to rescue homeless prostitutes and their children. Still, the illustration demonstrates a vision that is honorable and true. Persuasive leaders are honorable, just, and fair-minded and look for win/win scenarios. Great leaders are not only honorable; they also support honorable causes. They connect themselves to just causes that are good, beneficial, and point toward the greater good for society. They communicate to supporters how an organization raises the quality of life of others. This helps to build corporate morale.

Whether you sell photocopy paper, hygiene products, lug nuts, or trash bags, attempt to see the honorability in what you sell. If you lead teachers, assembly line workers, or non-profit volunteers, help your organization see the positive impact that it makes on its constituents and customers. Avoid comparing the morality of what you do to the cause of other organizations. Not every organization rescues prostitutes and their children from the streets. Instead, focus on how what you do changes the world for the better. Then like the donors and workers who gave money and volunteered their time, followers will come alongside and support you. Make your cause honorable. Visualize how it helps people and raises their quality of life. Then convey that to everyone around you. Persuasive leaders convincingly communicate the impact that their mission has on the world. When you do this, you won't have to plead with people to follow you. Instead, they will want to.

5. Encouragement

It was a cold day in Dallas, Texas. I left the hotel at seven in the morning, stopped by my favorite place for some green tea, and headed to the corporate offices of one of the greatest motivators of the twentieth century, Zig Ziglar. Zig's son, Tom, had invited me to make a motivational presentation during their webinar to over one thousand online viewers. When I walked in the door at eight I could hardly believe who I saw standing in the hallway. It was Zig Ziglar himself. The eighty-four-year-old internationally acclaimed motivational speaker looked at me and stretched out his hand in a warm greeting.

I introduced myself and said, "Mr. Ziglar, it's an honor."

To which he replied, "The honor is mine, Jason. Are you married?"

I said, "Yes sir."

"Good. Let me tell you the secret to a long-lasting healthy marriage." Then, without breaking eye contact he said, "Don't ever stop courting your wife." What a powerful, succinct statement. I've held onto that nugget since that morning of January 26, 2011. Now let me rewind the story and fill in the blanks for you.

Zig's biography is extensive. He addressed millions of people in live events over his long and prestigious career. He wrote more than thirty books and produced more than fifty different training and motivational audio programs. Even after his devastating fall down a flight of stairs in 2007 that left him with short-term memory problems, he continued to travel and speak through 2010.

When I met him that morning, he asked my name and remembered it throughout the entire conversation. When I said,

"Mr. Ziglar, it's an honor," his reply was, "The honor is mine," and I sensed he was sincere. Then he immediately turned the conversation to me by asking a question about my personal life and giving me some great advice. When I walked away, I felt appreciated and motivated to be a better husband. Why is that? Mr. Ziglar was an exhorter, and with his gifts and talents, he encouraged millions of people around the globe.

Mr. Ziglar understood that while leaders can train their people to do their jobs with excellence, motivating them will help staff reach their greatest potential. And motivated employees lead a business or organization to achieve its greatest potential.

Leaders who do not encourage, appreciate, or respect those they lead inevitably allow a cesspool of toxic attitudes to develop in their organization. Without encouragement, organizations tend to become negative. Eventually, people begin to gossip and complain. Bitterness and distrust set in, until finally members of the organization become highly self-centered. This drastically impacts organizational morale.

The goal of a persuasive leader is to guide people to transformational decisions. They not only train people, they motivate them. They are encouragers. They have the ability to look into someone's soul and transmit something that boosts his or her life. They lead people from a place of stagnation and frustration to a place where they believe they can move beyond anything that holds them back.

When leaders mentor their followers and show them appreciation, respect, and encouragement, it leads to trust, a sense of calling, and high morale.

Instead of hoping that people will automatically become positive, take the initiative and become a persuasive leader. Learn to train and encourage. Look for the good in those you lead, and highlight their positive traits. When you are not around those you lead, talk positively about them. Encouragement leads to respect, appreciation, and most importantly, trust. With these qualities in an organization, you will become the persuasive leader you're destined to be.

All of these traits—integrity, dedication, wisdom, honor, and encouragement—are good, but they are not enough. You need a sixth quality in order to reach your greatest potential as a persuasive leader. It's the sense of *calling*.

6. Calling

What is a calling? It is that golden thread we mentioned earlier. It's the work that you were born to do. It's that place that gives you a sense that you are exactly where you should be. When you find your calling you know that "I was wired for this; I was designed for this."

Confucius said, "Choose a job you love and you will never have to work another day in your life." I disagree. What if you're not any good at what you love? The American Idol tryouts are proof that many people love singing but can't make a living at it. NFL linemen wouldn't make good Olympic gymnasts despite their longings to do so. NBA players wouldn't make good jockeys either. I would love to fly a 787 Dreamliner, but with me in the pilot's seat you wouldn't expect to get to your destination in one piece. Too many people make the mistake of pursuing what they love and then trying to learn to do it well.

Instead, *do what you were wired to do, and then figure out a way to fall in love with that*. Don't fight who or what you are destined to be. Each of us has gifts and talents that will help us excel in certain areas. Figure out your golden thread, and focus your efforts on being the best you can in that area. That, my friend, is your calling.

Persuasive leaders are in touch with who they are destined to be. Leaders like Steve Jobs or Nelson Mandela may or may not have used the term *calling* when describing their work, but if you could ask them, I am sure they felt that all signs pointed them to the occupation they chose for their lives. Most of us are glad they paid attention to those signs.

In addition to knowing their own calling, persuasive leaders have a keen ability to help others identify their golden thread. They reach out to mentor others to reach their greatest potential in the areas in which they are gifted. They spot people who fit well in the organization and help them succeed. If someone doesn't seem to be progressing vocationally, a good leader who understands a calling will help that individual find a better path to where he or she needs to be.

All of these qualities—integrity, dedication, wisdom, honor, encouragement, and calling—help leaders move organizations toward a culture of high morale. Organizations can train their people in product knowledge, manufacturing, marketing, and technical skills, but they may find it difficult to raise morale. The only way to do so is by being the kind of person they will trust. When all of these traits flow together and you are seen as trustworthy, morale rises. When morale rises, productivity, efficiency, and profits follow.

Stay true to your calling. Don't be distracted by the plethora of causes in the world. Few are worthy of your undivided dedication. Stay focused on your golden thread. Help others reach their greatest potential. As you do, you will become someone people want to follow.

Become Someone People Want to Follow

Practical Steps to Becoming a Persuasive Leader

Before we close this chapter, I want to leave you with three ideas to help you in your quest to become someone people want to follow. Leading people is not for wimps. It's not easy. But few things are as rewarding as guiding a group of outstanding people toward a common goal, accomplishing that goal, and enriching lives in the process. Much of what happens in our lives takes place because we have a certain mindset; a perception that says it is possible to become an outstanding leader. Be open to the possibilities and try to imagine the great things that can happen in your life.

One way to develop your leadership skills is to *volunteer at a favorite charity*. Well-organized charities are always looking for volunteers. Nothing builds leadership qualities faster and more efficiently than working with volunteers. Unlike employees, volunteers serve at will. They are there because they support the cause. If you can learn to motivate volunteers, you will develop essential skills for leading people to transformational decisions.

Invest some time at a soup kitchen, homeless shelter, church, synagogue, or community center. Don't expect your experience to be easy, though. You'll discover that people usually place their careers, families, and other important commitments ahead of that for which they volunteer. Their service usually takes a back seat to everything else. So your patience and your commitment to being a leader will be tested. However, if you can persuade volunteers to follow you, you'll have the tools to motivate just about anyone.

A second way to develop your leadership skills is to *offer your services at no cost to a leader you admire*. Many great leaders wouldn't take on a student at any price. Their schedules usually prevent this. But learning from a great leader shouldn't cost him or her anything. This is especially true if you look for a way to serve that leader in an area where he or she has a need. While serving them, you'll be able to glean important lessons by observing how they respond to life situations.

When the opportunity presents itself, ask that leader, "What is one of the most important lessons you've learned over the years?" You might also consider asking, "If you could travel back in time thirty years ago, what advice would you give yourself to prepare for today?"

If you commit to serving an admired leader, be a person of your word. When individuals ask me to be their leadership coach, I always test them with an uncomfortable task to see how committed they are. Usually, I'll ask them to straighten out, organize, or clean something. One time, a young man offered to help in whatever area I needed in exchange for me being his speech coach. I said, "Great! Be here tomorrow morning at five. We are setting up the big tent that seats five thousand people. Bring your gloves, boots, and prepare to sweat." I never saw him again. Make sure you count the cost before you make the offer. Otherwise, doors to certain leaders will be locked forever.

A third idea for growing as a leader is to *make a no-strings-attached offer to someone you'd like to emulate*. Find out what gift they would want or what their interests are. This is not meant to be manipulative. Instead, you are seeking a way to brighten their day—nothing else. Find out what speaks to their heart and do something for them without expecting anything in return. You reap what you sow. Sow good things into the lives of leaders you admire and you will reap knowledge on becoming a leader people want to follow.

In this chapter, we talked about six traits of persuasive

leaders and the important role they play in their lives. We saw that integrity is the foundation for every great leader. Zig Ziglar sums it up well: "You can get everything money will buy without a lick of character, but you can't get any of the things money won't buy—happiness, joy, peace of mind, winning relationships, etc., without character."[2] Without integrity, it is impossible to lead people consistently to transformational decisions.

Dedication and commitment prove to your followers that you are willing to make the necessary sacrifices to move the cause forward. Supporters, workers, donors, and volunteers are reluctant to come alongside you until they are convinced you are fully committed to the vision of the organization.

Next, we discussed the importance of wisdom. We must work hard to become wise. Great leaders display thoughtful decision-making abilities and render their opinions with prudence.

Great leaders show the difference their organization is making in the world and how lives are enriched as a result of their efforts. Everyone wants to feel they are making a difference and persuasive leaders show their followers how they do just that.

Encouragement keeps organizations from slipping into a cesspool of pessimism and bitterness. One of the top reasons people quit their jobs isn't because of salary. It isn't because of inconvenient hours or poor working conditions. According to Forbes, people say they quit because they don't feel appreciated or respected.[3] They don't feel their leader listens to them. So, be an encourager. Highlight the positive. Look for ways to help your people remove the barriers that hold them back. Never gossip or talk negatively behind their backs, and don't allow others to do so either.

Finally, persuasive leaders know their calling. They have a clear idea of their golden thread. They have a sense of being called to do what they do. They also help others identify their golden thread because they invest time in those they lead. Stay true to your calling. Stay in alignment with your gifts. Don't waver or get caught up in other causes that do not clearly connect to your golden thread. Leaders who stay on message and on course lead people to transformational decisions. Doing so will help you become someone people want to follow.

Questions for discussion or personal reflection:

1. If you could do whatever you want with your life, what would you do? What gifts would you have? With whom would you work?

2. How many people would you want to impact? How much money would you make? How many children would you have? Where would you go, live, or visit?

3. What is your golden thread? What are your gifts and talents? What is the one thing in the world you could be the best at if the right doors opened for you?

4. What are some concrete steps you can take in order to become someone people want to follow?

5. What's the most important thing you've learned in this chapter?

Chapter 2

VISUALIZE WHERE PEOPLE NEED TO GO

"What in the world are you doing with your life?" my mentor asked me. Up to that point, I thought I was heading in the right direction. Suddenly his question caused me to doubt myself. He had always been supportive and insightful. This time he pushed me to the limit of my self-confidence. That was the point. He wanted me to discover what my true convictions were and why I believed what I did. *What* am *I doing with my life?* I asked myself. For a long moment, all I could do was look at him.

Have you ever asked yourself what in the world am I doing with my life? How about now? Are you satisfied with who you are, what you do, or where you are going? Regardless of the position you hold, you've probably wondered if the path you're on is the right one.

In this chapter, we'll look at the different traits that persuasive leaders develop. I see them as their sense of perception, vision, purpose, timing, and favor. Finally, we'll look at their ability to develop an effective plan. The first sense, *perception*, is the most crucial.

1. Perception

I landed at eleven in the morning in Buenos Aires, one of my favorite cities in Latin America. I cleared customs and met the driver just outside of baggage claim. As he drove me to the hotel where I would spend the next four days, there wasn't a cloud in the sky. I realized at that moment why they named the city "good air."

After checking into my hotel, I unpacked and headed down to the front desk. My mission was to find a quaint outdoor café and enjoy an espresso. The hotel representative asked me if I wanted a map. I kindly declined. *After all*, I thought, *who needs a map or a GPS when you have a good sense of direction?* He smiled as if he heard my internal conversation and said, "Fine. For your information, Mr. Frenn, there's a great café about ten blocks to the north," as he pointed to his left.

After walking ten blocks in the direction he gestured, I found a wonderfully situated coffee and pastry bistro with shaded tables on the sidewalk. I spent an hour enjoying a South American moment in the heart of a great city. As I paid the bill, I asked the cashier a simple question to ensure I wouldn't get lost. "Where is the Cristal Palace Hotel?" She replied, "Ten blocks west and two blocks south." I thanked her and walked out the door. It was about two o'clock.

Instead of retracing my steps back to the hotel, I decided to take a leisurely stroll. *Ten blocks to the west and two to the south, that's all I need to remember,* I thought. About forty-five minutes into my journey, I discovered that my internal compass was off. It wasn't slightly off; it was completely off. What I thought was north was really south, which meant that my east and west were wrong as well. As a result, for the first time in my adult life I was completely lost. Not only that, but the sun seemed to be going in the opposite direction than normal. It looked earlier in the day than the time I arrived at the café. I felt confused, disoriented, and frustrated.

I have lived all of my life in the northern hemisphere. The sun always follows a pattern in the southern sky. That's why

Visualize Where People Need To Go

moss grows on the north side of trees. Only during the last week in June does the sun come close to being directly overhead. Buenos Aires is further south than South Africa. For them, the sun is always in the northern hemisphere. So everything in my head was off by 180 degrees. I was embarrassed to have to ask directions five times that day. Each time someone gave me directions I said to myself, *That can't be right. West is in the opposite direction.* Finally, with great frustration and a sense of defeat, I hailed a cab and paid the fare for a short ride back to the hotel. I was using my northern hemisphere map (mental orientation), which doesn't work in the southern part of South America.

If you know how to read a map but you have the wrong map, you'll never reach your destination. If your orientation is off, you'll get lost. If you think north is straight ahead, but you're truly headed south, you will be forever frustrated. Eventually, you'll have to ask (or pay) someone to get you back on course.

Most people think that their problems are caused by external forces. Their perception tells them that other people or lack of resources hold them back. But most problems are internal, not external. Our destructive thought patterns or inaccurate maps cloud our emotional vision and keep us in the same harmful cycles.

That is not to say that our external problems or difficulties do not set us back. We all go through tough times, difficult scenarios, and relational challenges. The way we interpret things largely determines how or if we move forward. Our reactions to problems are heavily determined by our emotional navigational system. Much like a pilot who depends on his instrument panel to indicate nautical speed, altitude, wind, fuel level, and oil pressure, we depend on our navigational system to tell us if something is offensive, too hard, fun, depressing, or fulfilling. Our navigational system is wired to guide us toward what we believe is pleasurable and to avoid what is painful. What is our navigational system? In short, it is our perception. It's the way we interpret the world around us. It guides, directs, and advises us through the storms of life. It's the biggest factor that determines how we react or respond to problems.

Note that perception is not to be confused with perspective. There is an important distinction between the two. Perspective is a point from which we view something, figuratively or literally. It's the angle from which we see a house, building, sky, physical objects, personalities, problems, or situations. However, perception is how we interpret the data entering our mind from any given perspective.

There was a time when people initiated phone calls by talking to an operator. That operator, sitting at a switchboard, would take a cable assigned to the person who wanted to make the call and plug it into the socket that belonged to the person whom the caller wanted to call. Once in a while, the operator connected the caller to an incorrect recipient.

Now imagine an entire switchboard full of wires assigned to incorrect recipients. What you think is the correct recipient is someone entirely different. That is the precise condition of the navigational system (perception) for many people who are lost and have no idea where they are going.

When emotional wires get crossed in your mind, what you think is good and healthy isn't that at all. What you believe is fun may turn out to be harmful. What you think is an innocent indiscretion could turn out to be horrifically painful. If you struggle in your personal relationships, finances, career, and family, it may be because your perceptions are wired incorrectly.

Visualize Where People Need To Go

There are those who are affluent, famous, and seemingly fortunate, but they find it difficult to stop the craziness in their lives. How many times have we turned on the news to hear that another famous person has been arrested for drug possession or overdosed on narcotics? The emotional wires that built their perceptions greatly affected the way they saw life. Although they supposedly had it all, their perceptions guided them to destruction.

On the other hand, we see people coming from challenging socioeconomic conditions who overcome insurmountable odds to become highly effective business people, teachers, doctors, lawyers, authors, parents, and spouses. The difference between those who fall into destructive patterns and those who live healthy and meaningful lives isn't where they are situated in life (perspective), but how they view and interpret life (perception).

Those who desperately need a perception overhaul are most likely unaware that their interpretation of the world is tainted. They are not living life; instead, they're merely surviving it. As a leader, being in tune with your navigational system is important, but making it healthy is essential.

Your perspective (where you are situated in life) may be challenging at the moment. You may work with people who are hostile or rude. Perhaps you are stuck in poverty or in a highly dysfunctional home. Maybe your children are rebellious or your marriage is a disaster. You might have little education. The issue isn't how these things are affecting you, but rather how you manage them and respond to them. In order to form a more healthy perception, you must first embrace truth.

Persuasive leaders have an internal compass that shows them where true north is. When wading through a plethora of vocational and personal options, they manage to discover the best direction for their own life and help others find an effective way to accomplish what they need to accomplish. One of the most important ways they become effective leaders is by finding their own way first, by developing a healthy perception. The following three ideas will help you do the same.

First, there are certain absolutes that never change. Tell yourself every day that *failure is not a person*. Failure is an event, and yesterday ended last night. Each day is a fresh start. You have the freedom to choose what is right, healthy, and good for yourself and those you lead. Your most powerful asset is not money, people, or things. It's the way you think, and you can improve that anytime, anywhere. If you are alive, it's for a reason. Because of that purpose, you already have the potential to develop all the gifts and talents necessary to become highly effective in your golden thread.

Second, *go back to school*—literally or figuratively. Now, more than ever, education is effective, and in many cases it's free. You can study in your car listening to audiobooks or speeches. You can download thousands of books on a tablet or mobile device. iTunes University gives you access to higher education classes in some of the most prestigious institutions in the world.[1] Broadening your education opens your mind to the possibilities of something powerful and revolutionary. Your perception will transition from *it can't be done to there is a better way, and by taking the right steps, I'll find that way.*

Third, *surround yourself with people who lift you up* instead of tear you down. Feed your mind with thoughts that are healthy and uplifting, not venomous. Commit to friendships that are healthy and seek objective feedback from these people to pull you up to the next level. Share your most important goals with a select mature group that truly rejoices when they see you

Visualize Where People Need To Go

succeed. Look for a way to spend time with this group of people regularly, either in person or by telephone or social media.

Once your perception becomes clear, you'll have a clear vision of where you need to go. Regardless of the chaos, disruptions, or conflict you face, much like a pilot you'll effectively negotiate the storm.

2. Vision

The forty-five-year-old man was terrified. It was the first time that Ubaldo had been asked to give a speech. The crowd wasn't small; it was a multitude. Six thousand members of a multi-level marketing organization packed into a downtown arena and anxiously waited for him to tell his story. Two large projection screens, six cameras, hundreds of intelligent lights, lasers, and an immense stage made the evening the super bowl of sales events. He stepped up to the podium and extended his trembling right hand. He grabbed the microphone and began his presentation.

"As a child living in Mexico," he said, "I wandered the streets many times barefoot looking for ways to make money just to have a meal. I remember many years when there wasn't a single gift under the Christmas tree and many birthdays came and went without so much as a cake. My father died when I was two. My mother loved us but couldn't bear the burden of raising all nine of us. I immigrated to the United States in 1985."

After painting a raw and realistic picture of his humble upbringing, Ubaldo paused for a moment, then continued, "For years, my wife and I struggled to make ends meet. I couldn't find work, couldn't put food on the table for my family, or pay the rent. I vividly remember the worst day of my life. My wife had to take my children to live with my mother-in-law. It was humiliating. It was the ugliest feeling I ever had."

It was at his lowest point that Ubaldo suddenly had an epiphany. "If I could create a business that had no limits regarding the amount of people it could serve, then I would have no limit on the amount of money I could make. The more my organization could serve, the more it could help me provide for my family. That is when I decided to form a business with this organization. Within weeks, I set a goal to help five hundred people get a job so that they too could provide for their families. Many of you are the product of that vision." The crowd erupted into applause.

"The happiest day of my life is when I sent for my wife and kids," Ubaldo said. "They left in a car, but they came back to me on an airplane, thanks to a $3,000 bonus I received from my business. Since then, we've never had to live apart. And just as important, thousands of people here tonight don't have to leave their families either. Together, this past year, we sold $50 million worth of household goods to individuals and families and saved them thousands of dollars on those products. Together we helped 50,000 people join this organization and help them start their businesses. Together, we've helped families rediscover their dignity. And together, we're going to continue to change tens of thousands of lives forever. Thank you and God bless you!"

Ubaldo received a standing ovation that night. Why is that? His suffering produced an epiphany. His epiphany produced a vision. His vision produced actions. His actions produced results. His results produced a change in him, his family, and thousands of other immigrant Hispanics who were suffering as well.

Visualize Where People Need To Go

Why is having a vision so important for a persuasive leader? A vision is a mental picture of where you want to lead people. If your perception is healthy and clear, then your ability to see where you want to lead people will be clear. Henry Ford saw a world where his assembly lines produced a vehicle. Steve Jobs envisioned a world where cameras, music-playing devices, calendars, address books, games, credit cards, boarding passes, and millions of other items were digital and contained in one handheld device. NASA saw a space shuttle that could transport materials into space, return to earth, and launch again for future missions.

Some visions are not as concrete as these. Martin Luther King saw a world free from racial divide. Dietrich Bonhoeffer envisioned a world free from tyranny and social injustice. Jesus saw a world free from spiritual lostness, physical sickness, and wicked oppression. Every one of these visions turned into movements, but every one had a humble beginning.

Do you have a vision? If so, what is it? What is your promised land for those you want to help? How does your vision enrich other people's lives? If you could lead a group of people, regardless of its size, what do your convictions tell you is the best place to lead them? Whether you want to contribute something significant to people's lives financially, spiritually, maritally, familially, occupationally, hygienically, productively, educationally, or socially you must have a vision that clearly depicts what your promised land looks like when you arrive.

As a persuasive leader, you must have a vision of where you need to lead others. In order to develop a clear vision of where you want to lead others, take some time after you finish reading this chapter and write down your vision on a piece of paper or in your digital note pad. Visualize whom your vision helps and how the marketplace or social group will experience transformation as a result. Your vision should be a natural derivative of your golden thread. Once it becomes clear to you, then you can focus on the reason behind what you do.

3. Purpose

I sat across the table from Robert H. Schuller, the host of the international television program, *Hour of Power.* "I'm looking forward to hearing you as our guest speaker," he said. "Tell me, what is the title of your message?"

I said, "Well, I am vacillating between two different titles, but the one that I'm leaning toward is 'Your *why* must be bigger than your *but*.'" Dr. Schuller's look was classic. Somewhat puzzled he asked, "Excuse me?" Then I explained that *but* in this case is spelled with one t. "In other words," I said, "Your reason for doing something must be larger than any excuse that arises."

"I love it!" he said. "How did you come up with that?"

I went on to explain that in 1996 my life changed forever. Between August 1 and December 15 of that year I lost sixty pounds. My waist dropped from a size forty to a thirty-four. Whenever I speak in front of a group, inevitably people come up to me afterward and ask, "Tell me, what is your secret?" I tell them, "The *how to* is always secondary in importance to the reason *why* you do something." If your reason is strong enough, you will find a way to go where you want to go, buy what you want to buy, become what you want to become, or experience what you want to experience. A strong purpose will enable you to reach your goal.

"What was your *why* to lose all that weight?" Dr. Schuller

Visualize Where People Need To Go

asked. I explained that before I turned thirty, I went in for a complete physical checkup. After looking at my blood work and checking my blood pressure, the doctor gave me some horrific news. "Your blood pressure is 170 over 100 and your cholesterol is 290," the doctor said. "If you want to see your children have children of their own, you must get your life under control. If you want to live, you don't have a choice."

In a matter of seconds, I discovered a purpose for exercising, eating right, and taking care of my physical body. It was simply this: I want to live; I don't want to die. The next morning, I got up and started to exercise. Although it was difficult at first, I alternately ran ninety seconds and walked ninety seconds for a total of twenty minutes. I eliminated all fried foods and red meat from my diet. I didn't eat after six in the evening, slept for eight hours each night, and read books on health and nutrition. After several months, I was walking less and running more for a total of thirty minutes Monday through Friday. Each day, I run 2.5 miles. My cholesterol is low. My blood pressure is normal, and although I take medication, I am in better shape than I was in my twenties. Had I not discovered my purpose or my *why* and made the proper adjustments when I was younger, I might not have lived long enough to write this book.

Having a powerful reason to do what we do is what makes leaders great. Their *why* is powerful. It is strong. Their motive doesn't allow the excuses that arise to derail, distract, or detract them from moving forward. Wilbur and Orville Wright successfully paved the way for us to move from the era of horse and buggy to supersonic air travel. Facing a headwind of adversity, their reason to pursue aviation was stronger than any potential setback. The same could be said for the allied forces defeating Nazi Germany or the Japanese aggression in the South Pacific. Men and women laid their lives on the line for freedom. Their reason for doing so was greater than any intimidation or fear they faced. They discovered their purpose and helped others do the same.

Why do you do what you do? Why do you live the way you live? Why do you go where you go or work the way you work? Think about it for a moment. Now compare the reality of what you do, where you live, where you go, and the way you work to what you aspire to do, live, go, and work. Is there a difference? If so, you can change if you discover your purpose (why) and make it greater than any excuse (but). When you do you'll accomplish whatever you set your mind to do. No excuse will be able to prevent you from moving forward.

If you want to discover a powerful *why*, ask yourself the following questions:
- Who are the most important people in my life?
- What is the most important thing I do?
- Should I do something significantly different in order to preserve, cultivate, and nurture the important people in my life and the important things I do?
- What can I do to improve both of these areas?

When you discover a strong reason for change, you have a purpose. This is what motivates you. As you discover what motivates you in addition to what's important to you, when adversity intensifies, your commitment will keep you on track. Join the many great leaders who understand this principle. The discovery of your purpose will lead you to a better understanding of your destiny.

4. Timing

Don Judkins was born into a humble family. His parents divorced when he was four years old, and he never had a stable family life. He grew up without a consistent father figure because his mother had married five times. After graduating from high school, both he and his wife-to-be, Maxine, attended the same junior college located in the San Joaquin Valley in California. Both came from poverty.

Three weeks after their wedding, Don was laid off from his job as an apprentice clerk in a local market. The next day, he drove to Bakersfield and applied at another supermarket chain as an apprentice grocery clerk. The starting salary was $57 a week. They hired him on the spot. Financially, Don and Maxine faced many difficulties and challenges. For a period of time their diet consisted of a daily portion of canned tuna. Each can cost twenty-nine cents. According to Don, Maxine learned every way imaginable to prepare the canned fish.

Over time things improved greatly for them. For nearly two decades Don had a stellar career in the grocery business. After managing one of the most profitable regions in the grocery chain, something life-changing happened. The company fired him. Instead of interpreting that as a loss, he saw it as perfect timing for a major transition. After a short deliberation, the grocery chain realized their error and pleaded with Don to return, which he did for a year. However, the signs of transition in Don's mind were clear. He always had an interest in building houses, but he was too busy with the grocery business to learn how to use a hammer and nails. The apparent setback from his employer was a blessing in disguise. So he went to his stepfather, a builder, to learn how to frame a house.

He and Maxine had few assets to begin a construction company. Nonetheless, Don started his business fulltime April 1, 1976, at age thirty-nine. Thirty-seven years later it is estimated that he has built more than 3,300 homes, seventy-five apartment buildings, and many office buildings and four-plexes. Today Don is one of the most prominent developers in the San Joaquin Valley. He and his wife are multimillionaires and have put a roof over the heads of tens of thousands of families.

Don and Maxine Judkins came from great poverty and scarce resources, subsisting on crackers and tuna. However, their sense of timing is remarkable. Several years ago they started a family charitable foundation, and currently give away $1 million a year. Each time the real estate market surges, the Judkins have plenty of inventory. When the economy slows, they produce less and lower their prices so that their inventory moves quicker than those of other developers. That is one of the lessons Don learned early on in the grocery business. They capitalized on each major transition and have prospered, impacted people, and set a high standard for philanthropy. They have a sense of timing and direction that few people have.

I asked Don how he developed his sense of timing. His response was interesting, "Every time I check out what my competitors are doing," he said, "I ask myself if we can do it better and more affordably. More often than not, I am convinced we can. Knowing the best time to move forward is a combination of seeing the opportunity before it becomes obvious to everyone and doing it better than your competitors."

That's precisely why the Judkins have been so successful.

Then again I could tell you about another good friend, Klaus, who fled Nazi Germany and immigrated to America when he was six years old. Since the 1980s he and several other

Visualize Where People Need To Go

entrepreneurs have purchased radio stations across the United States. You might think that radio in North America hasn't changed much during that time. You would be correct. But the growth of Hispanics in the United States has been exponential. Over the years, Klaus and his business partners have built the largest Spanish-speaking nonprofit radio network in the world. The average listener to their network listens longer than those of any other network in the country, an average of nine hours a day. Who would have thought to establish a Hispanic network in the 1980s in America? Klaus did.

I asked Klaus how he developed his sense of timing. He responded, "I don't like to sit around waiting for life to happen. You have to seize the opportunity when it comes. Many people say they'll get involved in something when they have all the resources. There's only one problem. You never have everything perfect when you start something."

His answer is indicative of someone who understands that if you are going to impact the world around you, you must have a sense of timing. You cannot wait for change to happen.

John Wooden won ten national basketball championships in twelve years. Revered as one of the greatest college basketball coaches in history, Wooden sums up his philosophy this way, "When opportunity comes, it's too late to prepare."

Zig Ziglar says, "If you don't grab the oars of your boat and start rowing in the right direction, someone else will. And believe me, they will take your boat in the direction they want to take it. Waiting for all the traffic lights to turn green or all the chores to be finished or for life to produce the perfect scenario will cause you to wait for an eternity."[2] The perfect time to move forward comes around more often than you think. Be prepared.

As all persuasive leaders do, the people I've mentioned

above anticipated something great. They foresaw the moment well before it happened. They sensed where people needed to go before it became apparent.

Your sense of timing determines your effectiveness as a leader. It gives you a significant advantage in every area of life. Imagine sensing the best time to get in or out of the stock market. Imagine discerning the best time to move your place of residence, marry someone, attain a degree in a specific field, or approach a potential client. Imagine knowing the best time to change your career or when to ask for a raise. A good sense of timing tells us when it is safe to transition, share information, or simply stay put. Most importantly, it helps us effectively guide those we lead through their crucial decisions and to determine when those decisions will be most effective.

What can you do to develop the skill of better timing? How can you develop better discernment and learn to accurately anticipate the best moment to act? First, become an observer. Watch those who have mastered the skill you want to develop. Look for patterns in their behavior and take note of the moment when they take action. If you get the opportunity, ask them why they chose that moment to act.

Second, do what Don, Klaus, and Mr. Wooden did. See the need before it becomes apparent, and find a way to solve that need. Don't delay preparing for an opportunity until it comes your way. By then it'll be too late.

Third, spend time listening not to the pundits or talking heads but to yourself. Each of us has a still, small voice—a gut feeling. This voice can be one of your greatest assets. There are moments when that internal nudge or sixth sense is spot on. That is how the gift of timing communicates to us. So calibrate it. Hone it. Listen to your gut feeling, and do what you believe

Visualize Where People Need To Go

is conscientiously correct in the moment you feel is correct. Then you'll have one of the most important leadership skills that can be developed.

5. Favor

Jose was born into a middle-class home in Central America. He was a good son, a good student, and a well-mannered young man. One of his greatest passions was playing guitar in a rock band.

When I first met Jose, he was dressed in baggy jeans, a white t-shirt, a ball cap facing backwards, and sandals. He was scheduled to play guitar during an outdoor concert in the park. About fifteen minutes before the concert started, the owner of the audio company received a phone call. The sound engineer had been unexpectedly delayed and would arrive late. Jose overheard the conversation and said, "I can run sound for you, but I'll have to play guitar while I mix."

At first, the idea seemed absurd, but when the concert started, Jose stood over the soundboard and mixed with headphones over his ears, playing guitar with the band standing a hundred feet from him on the stage. He didn't play guitar perfectly, but the audio mix sounded professional. That day, he inadvertently discovered his golden thread. He displayed his gift to be able to mix audio in a live event so that it sounded natural and balanced.

Soon doors began to open for Jose to run sound for other bands in venues throughout Central America. The demand to play guitar diminished, but the need for a sound engineer continued to grow. Several years later, a sound studio in Mexico asked him to come on staff and record hundreds of artists and musical groups.

Power To Persuade

In May 2006, I held a large event in the Anaheim Convention Center arena with thousands of people in attendance. Inexplicably, the sound company couldn't make their own gear function. Jose was playing with one of the bands in the lineup of the event. When the sound company failed, Jose stepped behind the console and within fifteen minutes had the sound system working perfectly. The sound company was so impressed that they asked him to run sound for the two-day event.

Over the years, Jose continued to mix live sound in concerts, houses of worship, and special events throughout North and South America. He worked in recording studios in Mexico, the United States, and Central America. Although he still loves playing guitar both as a stage performer and a studio musician, he is fully dedicated to the one thing that sets him head and shoulders above many others. He is one of the best sound engineers I know. Today, doors open for him in the area of sound mixing. He has his own studio, travels internationally, and enjoys great favor in his area of expertise.

Have you ever met someone and thought that everything seems to go well for that person? It almost seems that every red light suddenly turns green for them. When things work without overwhelming resistance, the person has favor in a given area. Now I don't believe in magic, but I do believe that when we do the right things and work in harmony with our golden thread, things flow smoother. Effective and persuasive leaders who work in harmony with their golden thread find favor in their relationships, in business dealings, and in the eyes of those they serve. Their favor gives them a certain advantage. Persuasive leaders realize the areas in which they have favor and dedicate themselves to service in those areas.

Is there an area in which you seem highly gifted? Do

Visualize Where People Need To Go

people consistently say, "You do that so well"? It may be math, washing cars, or painting. It could be cooking, administration, sales, speaking, teaching, cleaning, or writing. It may be the imperative skill of being a parent. Your area of favor may or may not be your golden thread, but inevitably it will be tied to it.

For example, let's say that your golden thread has led you to work for the Red Cross. As a result, you find it easy to motivate people to volunteer and give financially. You may not be a fundraiser, but things come together for you more effectively than for others because this is your golden thread. As long as the task you embark upon is congruent with your golden thread, the tasks related to your function should work smoothly.

If new opportunities are not coming, doors are not opening, people are not supportive, or finances are continuously strained, take a realistic look at the area to which you are dedicating your life. You know you have favor when, generally speaking, things are working well financially, relationally, productively, and creatively. With favor, things flow for you naturally.

One of the gifts that persuasive leaders possess is the ability to help others see where they have favor. After all, the point of being an effective leader is to help others become all they can be, to help them reach their greatest potential. The only way to do that is to guide those who follow you to the areas where they will flourish financially, relationally, productively, and creatively as it relates to their golden thread.

6. A Plan

Imagine sitting on a flight heading to New York from Los Angeles. You take off at ten o'clock at night and are scheduled to arrive at six in the morning. You are a bit apprehensive, because there are reports of winter storms over the Rockies. Just after takeoff, the captain suddenly makes an announcement over the intercom:

> Ladies and gentlemen, welcome aboard. We're going to do things a little differently tonight. Instead of using our flight plan as mandated by the FAA, our GPS, or onboard navigational system, I've decided to simply fly east. I know that New York is on the East Coast so I am sure we'll get there sooner or later. Besides, the sun will be up in about five hours so we'll be able to see at that time. Now, sit back, relax, and enjoy the rest of your flight.

Tell me, what would be your gut feeling at that moment? Is that a flight you'd want to be on? Is that a pilot you would trust? Would you feel safe? Probably not, because the leader does not have a plan worth following.

Thankfully, no pilot of a commercial airliner would do this. Unfortunately, though, many leaders do this on a regular basis. They have no plan and execute that insufficiency well. They make up things as they go along and have no accurate way of measuring their progress. If they were pilots, they'd be fired immediately. Like Robert H. Schuller said, "If you fail to plan, you plan to fail."

Do professional sports coaches have a plan? Do generals have a plan? Do UPS or FedEx drivers have a planned route? Of course they do. Otherwise they would fail at their tasks.

Persuasive leaders do not make things up as they move forward. They have a plan. It might be a one-month, six-month,

Visualize Where People Need To Go

five-year, or a twenty-year plan, but they have a plan. They are highly effective at leading people to transformational decisions and effectively communicating their road map in the process.

So if you want to be a persuasive leader and lead tens, hundreds, thousands, or even millions of people to transformational decisions, first you must come up with a good plan. Define your goals. Articulate them. Make them clear so that even those who are not familiar with your business can grasp where you want to go.

Why is it so important to make your plan clear to all? Many times the people who come alongside to support you won't understand all the intricacies of your mission or business. All they care about is that you know where you are going and that there's a decent chance you'll get there. They need the assurance that you will reach your goals and that you are a person of your word. So allow them to understand your vision and get behind you. When they can see the validity of what you do and know your game plan for getting there, they will be much more likely to invest the resources you need to reach your goal.

Second, if you can see your vision, eventually your investors, supporters, clients, and followers will as well. If you can't, they won't. So be visual, concrete, and realistic. Visualize your goals and continue to simplify them.

Third, once you have your mission clearly defined, write down some significant and necessary milestones that you must reach along the way. Add to that how you intend to measure your progress and the individuals you need to team with in order to lead people toward the vision, your promised land.

The Essence of a Powerful Leader

I've discovered over the years that people often won't follow a leader to transformational decisions if that leader is missing something vital. A persuasive leader is powerful. Whether it's the power to persuade, the power to explain, the power to resolve, or the power to make someone feel secure, every great leader must exercise power in order for people to feel safe enough to follow. Far too many times, poor leaders leave their followers feeling disconnected, disoriented, confused, and floundering. In this chapter, we've learned how six areas are imperative in order to become the powerful and persuasive leader we desire to be. Here's a recap of those six areas.

First, in order to become a persuasive leader you need to have an adequate and healthy perception. Your perceptions should be clear and accurate in the area of your trade. Regardless of your educational level, how much money you have, or where you live, the lenses through which you see the world must be clean and not tainted. You improve your perception by changing the way you think, continuing your education, and surrounding yourself with those who will pull you up instead of tear you down.

Second, as a persuasive leader you must have a vision, a mental picture of where you want to lead people—your promised land. If your perception is clear, then your ability to see where you want to lead people will be clear as well. Write down your vision and visualize whom your vision helps. Then you'll be able to take the next crucial step in becoming a persuasive leader, developing your *why*.

Third, the *why* or purpose behind why you do what you do is the horsepower to accomplish the mission. If your *why* is

47

Visualize Where People Need To Go

strong enough, your *how to* becomes much less of a factor. Your why gives you the strength to overcome the obstacles that stand in your way. You can discover your why in any area by asking who are the most important people in your life and what is the most important thing you do. Ask yourself what can you do to preserve, cultivate, nurture, or bring change to those people and things.

Fourth, persuasive leaders have a great sense of timing. They display a gift of knowing when to walk through an open door, when to expand their business, when to make a strategic move, how long to stay, and when to walk away. Persuasive leaders do not wait for life to happen. You can develop your sense of timing by being prepared before opportunity comes, watching those who have mastered the skill you want to develop, and getting a good handle on your still small voice.

Fifth, favor is perhaps one of the most overlooked universal patterns that allow leaders to become highly effective. With favor, doors open without overwhelming resistance in a given area of our life. Things flow smoothly because everything works in harmony with our golden thread. Favor also serves as an indicator to help us stay congruent with where we are supposed to be and to stay focused on what we were designed to do. In order to identify your area of favor, ask yourself in what area do you seem highly gifted. Do others regularly mention that you do something particularly well? Your area of favor is inevitably tied to your golden thread.

Finally, great persuasive leaders know where they want to go, visualize where they want to go, and develop a plan to get there. No great leader worth following flounders through life without a plan. Develop your goals and articulate them in a rudimentary way. Then, come up with milestones and a way to measure your progress in reaching them.

As we conclude this section on persuasive leadership, I congratulate you on laying the foundation for developing the power to persuade. Some of your greatest breakthroughs will come as a result of what you are about to read in the pages that follow. The following section, "Persuasive Communication," will teach you some powerful skills to become a highly persuasive communicator. So turn the page, and let's continue this enriching journey together.

Questions for discussion or personal reflection:

1. Are you pleased with the direction in which you're heading? If so, what are you doing right? What needs to change? Is your perception healthy? Is your vision clear?

2. Do you have a vision? If so, what is it? What is your promised land for those you want to help? How does your vision enrich other people's lives?

3. What is your purpose? What are the excuses that hinder you from reaching your dreams, promised land, and important goals?

4. What is your area of favor? What would your spouse, friends, or parents say is your area of favor?

5. What's the most important thing you've learned in this chapter?

Section II

Persuasive Communication

Chapter 3

BECOME A POWERFUL COMMUNICATOR

"You can go where you want to go, do what you want to do, and be like you want to be." Those are the words of one of the great communicators of the twentieth century, Zig Ziglar. Your ability to communicate effectively largely determines whether or not you reach your goals. Your success is determined by whether or not you lead others to transformational decisions. That's what great communicators do.

How effective do you want to be as a communicator? How much of an impact do you want to make? Whether you are selling something, persuading someone, developing a company, acquiring capital, studying for the bar exam, getting married, or raising children, you must learn to become an effective communicator. How good you are in this crucial area directly determines how successful you'll be in your professional and personal life.

Great communicators enjoy something that others wish they had, a *connectedness* with themselves (internally) and with those around them (externally). They feel at peace with themselves and with the notion of sharing with others. The benefits of being connected, both internally and externally, allow great communicators to move beyond stagnation to a level of productivity and fruitfulness. If you have a genuine desire to be efficient and productive, then I believe you can learn the art of great communication.

This chapter is about you, the communicator. Chapter 4 will deal with the how-tos of great communication. We begin our discussion here with the first and most crucial area of communication, the *internal dialogue*.

The Power of Internal Dialogue

After being recruited by the Los Angeles Dodgers and playing one season in the minor leagues, my father was drafted into service in the Korean War. When he returned to the San Fernando Valley eighteen months later, he tended bar in my grandmother's Lebanese restaurant. That was the first year of his five-decade bartending career.

Like my father, my mother didn't attend college. She discovered her niche as a cashier for several car agencies. I watched both my parents work hard to make ends meet. I can't speak for the rest of the children of the world, but for me, it was difficult to imagine myself ever surpassing their accomplishments. Their successes and achievements formed my image of my future, the one I believed I was destined to fulfill. Don't misunderstand what I am trying to say. My parents always told me they believed in me. They said that I could become whatever I wanted to become. But other peoples' words don't mean a thing unless we take ownership and believe those words ourselves.

Less than a decade ago, the image I had of myself as a child was coming true. My wife and I had no money, no home, no vehicles, and no assets aside from a modest retirement account. Both of us had one important thing, a master's degree. Like our parents, we always worked hard and tried to live within our means. Still, there was a constant conversation going on in my head. It said, *your parents struggled to make ends meet. They never had financial security. Odds are, you won't either.* Up until the age of thirty-seven, I felt that my life was on course to live paycheck to paycheck. If I were fortunate, I would retire with a Social Security check and enough money in the bank to maintain my standard of living.

However, I kept hearing stories about immigrants coming to the United States and making millions of dollars. I watched people overcome insurmountable odds to purchase homes, put their kids through college, and travel where they want. Zig Ziglar said on several occasions that immigrants are much more likely to become millionaires than those raised in the United States because they haven't believed all the bad press about the economy in the news. That's when I decided to stop entertaining the thoughts that kept me bound and stuck in the same place. *If I can change the way I think,* I thought, *I can change my life and my destiny.* This was one of the biggest turning points in my life.

I wrote down what my thoughts should be. Instead of saying to myself, *Boy, I sure hope I can get ahead in life, own a home, and earn enough to help my girls through college,* I wrote down that I am getting ahead, that I am in the process of owning a home, and that I am earning money to help my girls through college. I learned that the most important conversation in my life was the conversation in my own head.

Most people do not understand how important their internal dialogue is. Either they entertain thoughts they shouldn't, or they ignore the thoughts they should be embracing. That's precisely why they are stuck and never go where they want to go, do what they want to do, or become who they want to become.

I discovered over the years that what we accept as truth is programming, which is a form of deliberate learning. Learning

Become a Powerful Communicator

forms our thoughts. Thoughts then produce our beliefs. That's why we go to school. We learn from our teachers how we should solve problems, research, and philosophize. Once we are convinced that we have truth, our thoughts turn into beliefs. Beliefs then produce feelings. We become emotionally attached to our beliefs as they become convictions. Once you have convictions about something, then you're well on your way to victory. Why? Feelings that become convictions produce actions. Ultimately, actions produce results.

I began to rewrite the scripts in my head and my internal dialogue. In the last ten years, the results have been wonderful. You are reading my sixth book. I speak to approximately 150,000 people each year at live events. Our daughters are almost finished with college without school loans, and yes, we were able to buy a home. Our cars are not new, but they are paid for. There are many other things I could credit for these accomplishments, such as timing, wisdom, and of course, God. If the conversation in my head had been left unchecked, perhaps I would have been blinded by my pessimistic attitude and missed the opportunities that came my way. Don't miss out on a great life simply because the conversation in your head is distorted.

The first step in becoming a great communicator is to prescribe a healthy conversation in your head. Like a doctor, you need to write out a healthy dose of thoughts. Think about the important qualities you seek and begin to claim those qualities for yourself. It is helpful to think of things you can say to yourself on a daily basis to help reprogram your thoughts.

Once you finish this chapter, take a piece of paper, copy the following sentences, and add to this exercise any additional qualities you want to claim in order to attain the healthy self-image you need. This will help you become what you're destined to be and establish the first step in becoming a great communicator.

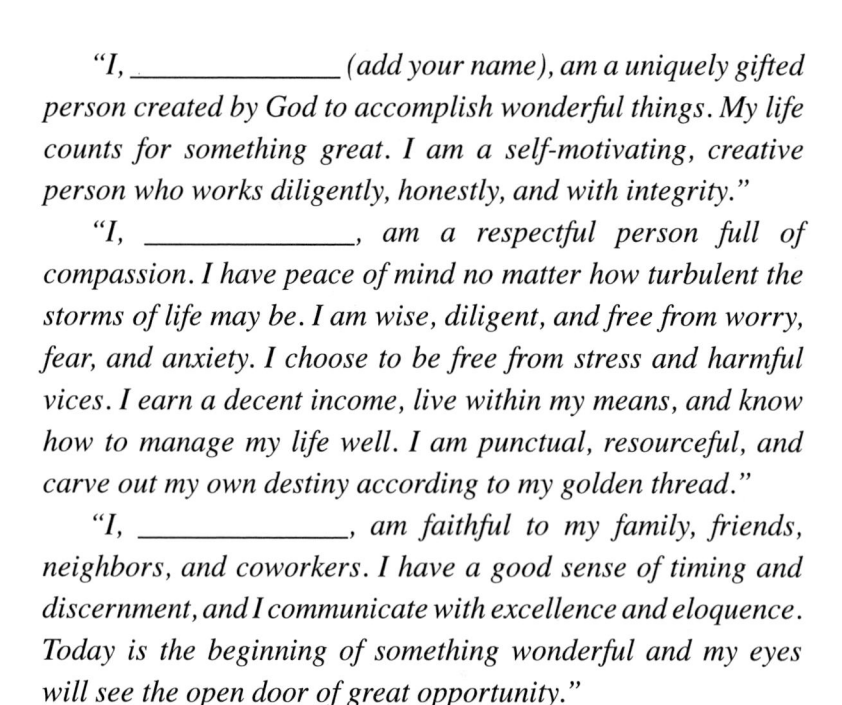

"I, _____ (add your name), am a uniquely gifted person created by God to accomplish wonderful things. My life counts for something great. I am a self-motivating, creative person who works diligently, honestly, and with integrity."

"I, _____, am a respectful person full of compassion. I have peace of mind no matter how turbulent the storms of life may be. I am wise, diligent, and free from worry, fear, and anxiety. I choose to be free from stress and harmful vices. I earn a decent income, live within my means, and know how to manage my life well. I am punctual, resourceful, and carve out my own destiny according to my golden thread."

"I, _____, am faithful to my family, friends, neighbors, and coworkers. I have a good sense of timing and discernment, and I communicate with excellence and eloquence. Today is the beginning of something wonderful and my eyes will see the open door of great opportunity."

Why is changing your internal dialogue so important? After a time of claiming these qualities, you'll begin to feel connected with what you are saying, and then you will begin to act in a manner consistent with those feelings and convictions.

Great communicators enjoy a feeling of harmony with themselves and with those around them, especially in their trade. It is difficult to communicate with confidence and security if you feel insecure or uncertain. How are you going to persuade others if you are not persuaded? So, first resolve the internal dialogue before you attempt to persuade your external audience.

Zig Ziglar, one of my mentors in the area of communication, shares a story on his website about the importance of forming your internal dialogue. Ziglar spoke to a large group of people in Salt Lake City on September 13, 1997. At the end of the long night, he signed books. One woman who asked for an autograph had such a compelling expression on her face that he knew he had to listen to what she had to say. This is what he writes about that meeting:

> She shared with me that when she got the self-talk card that was included in one of my audiotape programs, she couldn't even read the first list of qualities that she was supposed to claim.
>
> Throughout her life she had been so beaten down by her family and husband, that it was impossible for her to believe that she had the character and success qualities [listed on the card]. It took two or three weeks of listening to the tapes to build herself up to the point where she could look herself in the eye and claim that she was an honest, intelligent, goal-setting person. She continued to claim additional qualities until she could go through the entire list of 60-plus positive qualities. As a result, her demeanor and attitude changed dramatically. She started standing up straight, smiling, and even laughing.
>
> Then something truly fascinating happened. Her husband watched her new attitude emerge and [thought that] claiming the qualities could do the same for him. He started claiming the qualities and he, too, started to change. "He especially changed in the way he treated me," the woman told me. "Today we're getting along

better than ever and are happier than we've ever been."

...

The most important opinion you have is the opinion you have of yourself, and the most important conversations you will ever have are the conversations you have with yourself. The reality is that you cannot consistently, consciously claim all the qualities on the self-talk card without changing.[1]

Listen to the conversation in your head. Is it positive? Does it have a tone that lifts you up and says you can make it? Does it say you can go wherever you want to go, do whatever you want to do, and be whoever you want to be? Or is your internal conversation negative? Does it tear you down and paint a bleak picture? Each of us has an internal dialogue that reflects our self-image and attitude. If our internal thoughts are positive, that is projected to our external audience. If they are negative, that is what we reflect to others. By changing the way you think, you can change your life and destiny.

Once your internal communication is healthy and clear, then you can move on to the next quality that every great communicator must have. It is called the *transference of feeling*.

The Power of Transference of Feeling

After writing the book *Power to Change*, I researched the most effective ways to elevate sales and push my first book to the center of the marketplace. Through my research, I came across a website that hosted an event called the "Publicity Summit" in New York City. At the time, I had no clue who Steve and Bill Harrison were or what their organization did, but

Become a Powerful Communicator

I was intrigued by their concept of meeting one hundred of the top media producers in television, radio, Internet, magazines, and newspapers over a three-day period. Their philosophy was simple. If you can get enough publicity, there is no limit to how far your message will go.

I signed up for the "Publicity Summit," and gladly paid the fee that included the necessary training for the three-day event. In the months leading up to the summit, Steve Harrison had conference calls, training sessions, and individual consultations with the attendees.

I met the producers of the top four television networks, many radio shows, and magazine editors. I landed some great interviews and learned more about marketing in three days than in many classes I've taken on the topic. At the end of the summit, Steve Harrison asked the attendees to stay about forty-five minutes so that he could present another program called "Quantum Leap."

Over the previous three days, Steve delivered everything and even more than what he promised for the summit. During that final session, he looked at us and said, "I really want you to make it. Some of you have a great message and with some tweaking, your message will impact many people. I'm convinced." I could tell he meant it. Steve didn't just have a feeling. He had a conviction, and he managed to transfer it to us. We felt his passion, his desire, and his belief that Quantum Leap was the necessary next step for our training as people who wanted their message to reach the world. We began to feel about his Quantum Leap program the way he did. Of course, I signed up, and I'm glad I did.

Truthfully, getting me to sign up for his second program was one of the most difficult sales anyone could have made.

It wasn't cheap. But Steve conveyed to me that he understood my desire and aspiration to get my message out to a greater audience.

You see, an effective sale is nothing more than a transference of feeling. If you are going to convey a feeling to someone regarding an item, idea, or person, you must effectively communicate the way you feel about it. Steve was convinced, and the way he communicated his feeling was not manipulative. Once I felt his conviction that he had the solution to my problem, I signed up.

Whenever we sell, persuade, and especially communicate, we transfer the way we feel about something to the individuals with whom we are speaking or to whom we are writing. Persuasion is nothing more than a transference of feeling. When your customers, clients, spouse, children, friends, and colleagues begin to feel the way you do about something, you are persuading them. Once persuaded, they are much more likely to take action.

On the other hand, insincere persuasion is manipulation. Sooner or later, people see through disingenuous attitudes, and once your reputation is tarnished, it is highly difficult to gain back credibility. So when you write or speak with the intention of convincing someone to take action, be genuine. Be sincere. Being a person of integrity will gain you more sales, open more doors, reap you more benefits, gain you more favor, and win you more friends than the most creative, skillfully mastered manipulative plan in the world.

Another important point to remember is that unless you're in the business of selling planes, trains, sophisticated medical devices, medications, supercomputers, or a high priced specialty item, you should own the product you're trying to sell. If you're giving advice to someone in a blog, you should live by your own advice. It pains me to see a stockbroker giving stock recommendations on a financial news network only to discover at the end of the interview that he doesn't own any stocks. A car salesman who drives a different type of car than the one he sells has little chance of selling me one of the vehicles on his lot. And above all, I refuse to have an overweight medical doctor who smokes give me advice on healthy living. Why? None of these individuals believes enough in their own advice, nor have they have been changed as a result. They may be telling the truth, but their inconsistency strongly discounts their credibility and their ability to communicate with persuasion.

When I've asked people why they don't follow their own advice or why they don't own what they sell, many respond by saying, "Oh, I would, but I can't afford it." Or, "I'm not in the market." Therein lies the problem of communication. If persuasion is a transference of feeling, then what they sell or recommend is clearly not good enough. It's not worth the sacrifice. It's not the perfect solution. So before you try to persuade someone to take your advice, buy your product or follow your own advice. Once you do, you demonstrate to potential customers that you are convinced you have the best solution.

Many times, I am asked to raise funds for a nonprofit organization. Before I agree to help, I ask myself if I am willing to give the organization money for their charitable work. Before I ask anyone to give a dime to the organization, I write a check. This simple act demonstrates that I am convinced it's a worthwhile investment, and it gives me authority to ask others to give.

The Power of Seeing the Invisible

The first time I spoke to a group of people I was terrified. As a freshman in high school, I walked to the front of the class with my knees shaking. My palms were sweating. My heart was racing. My mouth was dry, and my tongue stuck to the back of my throat. To make matters worse, the other students, mostly seniors, hated the class. They endured the pain because it was a convenient way of fulfilling the English requirements before graduation. And if that wasn't enough, the teacher was the most demanding member of the faculty.

I placed my notes on the podium, cleared my throat, and before I could utter the first word, one of the upperclassmen sarcastically snorted, which caused an avalanche of other seniors to chime in with subdued laughter. The teacher never looked in their direction. He simply stared at me, waiting for my first words. In an attempt to lubricate my mouth, I intentionally swallowed, forcing my Adam's apple to move up and then down again. I took a deep breath, opened my mouth, and paused a few seconds. Just before I spoke the first word, one of the students whispered, "Come on, dude," forcing another extended pause.

Finally, I coughed out my first sentence. "Being up here is not the most embarrassing moment in my life," I said. "My most embarrassing moment happened two weeks ago." Then I went on to tell a story that I hadn't shared with others until then.

I had just walked out of church Easter morning at the community center in Big Bear City, California. It was overcast, thirty-eight degrees, with a slight breeze blowing across the parking lot. Separating the community center from the parking lot was a small wooden bridge. During that time of the year, the snow melted and a stream of ice water flowed through the park and headed toward the lake. The small river was about eighteen inches deep and eight feet wide.

My neighbors had invited me to join them for Easter Sunday morning service. They had two boys my age who loved football. So before we climbed back into their vehicle to head home, they grabbed a ball and started to play catch. Then the father said to his oldest son, "Go long, John." John took off, jumped over the river, and nearly slipped. Yet in spite of his near disastrous calamity, he made a marvelous catch. Then the their dad said to me, "Go long, Jason." I bolted toward the river knowing that I was quicker, more agile, and more skilled than John to fly over icy park streams. My timing was impeccable. My foot spacing was perfect. My speed was unmatched. The river was twelve feet away. I knew I had two full strides before I had to plant my launching foot as close to the water's edge as possible.

I flew down the gentle slope and spotted the perfect location to place my foot before propelling myself over the eight-foot stream. Traveling at fifteen miles per hour, I planted my foot three inches from the water's edge, and with every ounce of power I had I pushed off to gain as much height as possible. That's when I noticed a major malfunction. The soil at the edge of the river was pure mud. It provided no traction. Instead of launching like an Olympic athlete, my foot skimmed across the freshly buttered ice-rink-like surface. Suddenly, I found my feet out-accelerating the rest of my body. It was as if they figured that not every member of my body was going to make it to the other side of the river. So they were determined to make it first.

I will never forget the awkward sensation of rotating 180 degrees mid-flight so that I was now facing the river horizontally. When I finally crashed, my landing was perfect—a perfect bellyflop into the river. Even in eighteen inches of water, I managed to drench myself.

I immediately shot out of the freezing water and screamed, "IT'S COLD!" At that moment hundreds of people were exiting the community center, pointing at me and laughing hysterically. The timing couldn't have been worse. My landing couldn't have been more tragic. The water couldn't have been colder. My humiliation couldn't have been greater.

With that, I looked at the class and said, "That was my most embarrassing moment," which also happened to be the title of my speech. The students stared at me like a dog that had just heard a weird noise. The teacher had an almost undetectable smirk on his face. For five long seconds, I waited for a hint of laughter or even a courtesy clap from the audience. Nope, only crickets. Finally, I headed back to my desk thinking to myself, *I take it all back. This is the most embarrassing moment in my life.* The teacher's poker face did not reveal that he would give me an A, but he did. And the seniors never poked fun at me again. You never know for certain what an audience is thinking.

While it's true no one laughed or indicated they liked my presentation, there was one golden nugget that I discovered through the whole ordeal. Once I started telling them the story, I could see it. It was as if I was in a movie theater watching my story develop for the first time. Because I could see it, my classmates could see it as well. This is one of the great secrets to effective communication. Persuasive communicators see what they communicate to others. I call it *seeing the invisible.*

If you can see it, your audience can see it. If you can't, they won't. If you love something, appreciate someone, feel strongly about a life-changing principle, let people see it in your eyes. If you feel it, they will too. If you see the narrative develop before your eyes, your audience will as well.

I've sat through hundreds of presentations, heard thousands of speakers, and dealt with countless salespeople. I've also read hundreds of books, seen hundreds of plays, studied countless philosophers, and watched over five hundred movies. In all these experiences, I've seen that the best communicators see what they are saying. They visualize it and express it with the same enthusiasm they had the first time they experienced it. This is true in speaking and in writing.

This is what I do whenever I give a keynote speech, write a presentation, or ask someone to make a transformational decision. I pretend there's a movie screen superimposed upon the audience. While I am speaking to them, I watch the story develop on the movie screen, and I describe for them what I see. I feel the icy needles of the cold water. I hear the laughter of those leaving church. I feel the humiliation of being drenched from head to toe. I sense the awkward silence of the seniors sitting in the back row and the unclear signals coming from a stoic communications teacher.

Whether you are joining someone for a cup of coffee, writing a blog on your tablet or laptop, sharing a product in someone's living room, or standing in front of eighty thousand people in a stadium, try to see the invisible. Visualize what you are saying. As you prepare, go over it again and again until it plays before your eyes like a movie. At that point, you will be ready to communicate what you see to your audience.

Once you can see the invisible, you need to carefully and artfully construct the heart of your presentation, speech, or essay, that is, you need to have a point.

The Power of the Point

I stepped out of the Boeing 737 and walked down the jetway toward the terminal. All I could think about was getting to the venue on time. My plane landed an hour late, the event had already started, and they were going to announce me as the speaker in thirty minutes. My brisk walk turned into a slow jog and finally into a full-stride sprint. I ducked into the men's room, found the cleanest stall, and changed my clothes.

My wife was waiting for me at the curb. I threw my luggage in the trunk and jumped into the front seat while she drove. *Five thousand people waiting for me at the convention center,* I thought. *Is my PowerPoint and video ready? Is the book table set up?* Thousands of questions bombarded me. Every detail of my keynote speech had to come together perfectly.

I was prepared to make my presentation and I arrived on time. Did I know what I was going to say? Technically, yes. Was I emotionally prepared to say it? That was doubtful. The pressure of editing my content, reshaping my delivery, remembering to look into the television cameras, making sure my appearance looked natural (and not like I had just rushed back to my hometown after a five-hour flight), and coordinating a book launch all packed into my largest public address of the year turned my emotional equilibrium on its ear.

Two minutes before I walked onto the stage, my wife stood in front of me and picked a loose hair off of my shoulder. Then she slid her hands down my shoulders toward my elbows, looked me in the eye, and said, "Just remember the point, sweetheart." *She's right,* I thought. *All I need to do is remember the point. Everything else is secondary.*

Too many times we feel the pressure of accomplishing ten

things at once, and in the process, we forget the most important thing, *the point*. It's true in marriage, parenting, the law, sales, marketing, distribution, politics, and business. The point is what matters. When we fail in these areas, many times it's because we forget the point. The point helps us stay on message. It helps us maintain clarity and stay focused on our mission. It keeps us tied to our golden thread, what we were made to do or be.

When we make a sales presentation, a keynote speech, or lay out reasons someone should invest in our business, we can mistakenly make too many points. And in the process, we bury the most important one. Even worse, some communicators never clarify any point. They ramble on, hoping that something might stick. However, great communicators know that there is only one point. Everything else is meant to support that point. There may be several objectives along the way, but the best communicators plan and clarify the one thing they want their audience to say to itself when it heads out the door. They want their readers, clients, or potential customers to take something away from the encounter. Whether it's an action step or a decision, they want people to think that their life was changed because of the one thing that was said during the encounter or presentation. They want their audience members to come to transformational decisions. For example, "Today I discovered that my dream is possible." Or, "I am convinced that the solution I just read about is the best one for my situation."

Think about the most influential communicators you know of. They make their points crystal clear. Their audience knows exactly what they are saying. Whether authors, orators, kings, queens, or prophets, they lead their followers to transformational decisions by making their point concrete and easily identifiable.

So how do you make your point straightforward, simple,

coherent, and comprehensible? The answer is one of the best-kept secrets in the art of communication. The next section of this chapter will revolutionize your ability to hold an audience in the palm of your hand and drive home your point. If you are going to become a great communicator, persuade thousands, and lead people to transformational decisions, you must learn the art of telling the story.

The Power of the Story

I sat in the modern boardroom of one of the most respected nonprofit organizations in North America. They had asked me to advise them on fundraising, something I was glad to do. My phone was set to vibrate, as is customary when I'm in meetings. Still, the mild sound of three continuous text messages vibrated through my suit jacket. One of the board members glanced across the finely crafted oak table from his leather wingback chair. I looked on as if nothing happened. Then I inconspicuously slipped my hand into my pocket and squeezed the power button to ensure that the phone wouldn't make another sound. Finally, the meeting was over.

After a few pleasantries and courteous goodbyes, I turned my phone on only to discover the three text messages were from my wife. They read, "I know you're in a meeting, but please call me." Then, "Call me, please!" Finally, "Please call!!!" So I did.

"Honey, what's the problem?" I asked.

"Today I witnessed three miracles," she responded with a sense of restraint.

"Really?" I asked.

"Yes, really."

"Tell me what happened."

"I heard a strange noise coming from the living room," she said. "I knew the dog was downstairs so I wasn't concerned that someone had broken into the house. I walked down the stairs and couldn't believe my eyes."

Then for three long seconds, my wife didn't say a word.

"What?!" I demanded.

Then she said, "Do you remember what we did this past weekend?"

I said, "A lot of things. Please refresh my memory."

"We traveled to that small conference up the coast."

"Oh yes, I remember. But what does that have to do with this?"

She said, "Well, you remember the several hundred dollars in cash we made at the book table?"

"Yes," I impatiently responded, "but what does that have to do with the noise in the living room?"

"Well, when I walked downstairs I saw Maggie (our seventy pound shepherd mix puppy) standing in the middle of a pile of cash eating three twenty dollar bills."

"What?" I screamed. "How did she manage that?"

"I had a deposit in an envelope in my purse ready to take to the bank. She climbed on top of the dining room table, pulled my purse onto the floor, and ripped open the envelope. When I rounded the corner, she was eating twenty dollar bills."

"I'm sorry," I said. "You said something about seeing miracles?"

"Yes, well, the first miracle was that Maggie can't fully digest American currency. So within a minute, she puked them up."

I said, "Uh-okay. What was the second miracle?"

"Banks still accept half digested American currency."

I said, "That's good news. Gross, but good news. What was the third miracle?"

Confidently and authoritatively she said, "I did NOT kill the dog!"

I learned a valuable lesson that day. Never, under any circumstances _____!

Friend, in just a moment, I will fill in the blank for you. Before I do, however, do I have your attention? Do you want to know what my point is?

When you've mastered the art of telling stories you can share a personal story or one that is related to your topic, and with a slight edit make any point you want. For example, I could say that I learned a valuable lesson that day. Never under any circumstances leave your money unattended, or leave your dog alone with things that are valuable, or think your money is safe even if a guard dog is protecting it. There are many things I could emphasize with this story, but the point that I always emphasize is *your money is never safe*.

You can be a great storyteller and never set out to be a communicator, but you cannot be a great communicator without being a great storyteller. I've heard the best English and Spanish communicators of the twentieth and twenty-first centuries on two continents. Some are writers. Some are speakers. Others are presenters. I know preachers who speak to thousands of people each week, but as life-changing as their sermons may be, their messages are mediocre at best if they haven't learned to tell stories effectively. Politicians can wax eloquently for hours, but only those who can share a powerful testimony have lasting impact. Educators can teach, professors can lecture, and philosophers can write volumes, but only those who can effectively illustrate their point utilizing stories will impact their audience in a transformational manner.

The biggest section in bookstores is not self-help. It's not travel and leisure. It definitely isn't history or philosophy. It's fiction. Why is that? Since the beginning of time, the world has been enamored of stories, and it will be for the foreseeable future. Think about it. Movies are stories. Plays are stories. Musicals are stories. Television sitcoms, dramas, and soap operas are all stories. All children's books are stories. The most memorable parts of the Bible are all stories. So, friend, learn to tell stories effectively, and you'll set the stage for leading your audience to transformational decisions.

I believe this so profoundly that I began each section of this book with a story. Stories give credibility. They set the stage and contextualize. They illustrate the point, and take your audience on a wonderful and unforgettable journey.

People may or may not remember the five points in your hour-long presentation. They may or may not remember the thesis of your article. Most likely, they will not retain fifteen percent of what you say. But they will remember your stories, and if you effectively tie those stories to your point, you'll have a powerful impact.

So how do you become a good storyteller? How can you effectively use the power of story to lead people to transformational decisions? First, begin with your biggest asset, the story you know best. Start by sculpting your *signature story*. The signature story is your narrative. It's the one narrative you tell better than any other and better than anyone else. It tells your audience how you got to where you are in life.

When you tell your signature story, describe the *before*. Every listener wants to know what life was like before transformation took place. Often this includes a brief summary of your family life growing up. It might also touch on the adversity you faced before change occurred.

Then, describe the *transformational moment*. Every listener wants to hear what it was like when you experienced an aha moment, a change, or breakthrough.

Then, describe the *after*. Your audience wants to hear how your life has been revolutionized as a result of what took place, the product you used, or your paradigm shift. The listener yearns to hear how your relationships, health, feelings, and direction in life have all changed.

Finally, explain how what happened to you can transform the listener's life. When you share your signature story and say, "If my life can change as a result of _____ (fill in the blank), your life can change too," you will impact many lives. That is the function of a signature story.

Keep in mind that great stories have all of the following ingredients: credible introduction, setting or context, plot, problem, development of characters, dialogue (even if it's internal), change from past to present tense, a point, and a strong close.

As I explained earlier in this section, one of the great byproducts of a story is that each listener or reader extracts the point he or she needs. I can't tell you how many times people have read something I wrote or heard me speak at a convention and said, "I could really identify with what you were saying." Then they will mention something that I never said. Sometimes I wonder if they were reading a different author or were in another convention hall. Why is that? Readers, listeners, and audiences in general have a habit of extracting what they need when they need it.

The most effective stories reveal our weaknesses. When we share illustrations, stories, or anecdotes that portray us as superstars without opposition, the audience doesn't identify with us. People like to see us succeed, but they want to see the struggles, barriers, and challenges we faced in order to overcome. Audiences like to root for the underdog. So if your story shows how you overcame difficulty, it will inspire them, motivate them, and lead them to transformational decisions. What all audiences want are people who are real and characters with whom they can identify.

Audiences particularly enjoy stories in which the main character is imperfect, makes mistakes, and seems like a clown or even a buffoon. This works especially well when you, the narrator, tell stories of how you made it in spite of yourself. Illustrations and stories that indicate your humanness are great tools to help people come to a life-changing decision. They think if that person can overcome the odds, there's hope for me.

You might be saying, "I am not a speaker. I'm not a writer. Why in the world do I need to learn to tell stories?" The greatest persuaders will write, speak, or present in some way or another. You cannot persuade without sharing a testimony of how the solution you're offering changes lives. So if you want to lead people to transformational decisions, the most powerful tool you can use is the example of those whose lives have been revolutionized by your ideas or products.

Practical Steps to Become a Powerful Communicator

Every time you gesture, pause, speak a word, or simply keep quiet, you say something. You communicate all the time. Effective persuasion entails several important qualities.

Power To Persuade

As a persuasive communicator who leads people to transformational decisions, your internal dialogue needs to be confident and secure. If not, your customers, clients, or audience will detect your doubts and insecurities. It also means that you effectively transfer the way you truly feel about what you are selling or presenting. If you do not feel sincere and positive about what you present, you are a manipulator. The product or idea may be the correct one, but if you are not convinced, you are lying to yourself and to your audience. You must be sold on what you're selling.

As a great communicator, you see the invisible whenever you speak or write. You paint a picture with your words and create a journey for your customers, clients, or those you're trying to reach. If you can see it, you audience will as well. Also, having a point is absolutely essential. Make sure your point is relevant, insightful, and resourceful. Finally, utilize the most powerful tool the greatest communicators in history have used, the story. You can be a great storyteller and never set out to speak or write. But you can't become a great communicator without having the foundation of being a great storyteller.

Let me recommend a few resources to help you reach your greatest potential as a communicator. First, if you want to be a great speaker, find yourself a great speech coach. Tiger Woods has golf coaches. Joe Montana and Michael Jordan had athletic coaches and trainers. Every great political leader has advisers. So if the greatest achievers in just about any field have coaches, mentors, or advisers, why would you think you don't need one? Whether you are a sales representative, CEO, lawyer, manager, or business owner, find someone who can pull you up to the next level as a communicator. I have a speech coach, an editor for my writing, and an account with Survey Monkey so that I can solicit feedback regarding my communication.

Second, I highly recommend that you attend a storytelling seminar. These seminars will help you learn the art of thinking and communicating in story. There are organizations such as the National Storytelling Network (www.storynet.org) that can teach you to become a better storyteller.

Third, check out Toastmasters International (www.toastmasters.org), a great organization that has chapters in many cities around the world. You will pick up great tips and learn something new every time you gather to practice your communication skills.

Fourth, the National Speakers Association (NSA) (www.nsaspeaker.org) is an organization comprised of speakers around the United States and certain countries of the world who gather to learn from the best communicators of our day. NSA provides comprehensive resources and education designed to advance the speaking skills of its members. The yearly fee is not cheap, but if you are interested in developing your skills in presentation, NSA will help you move forward in this crucial area.

Fifth, the Ziglar Corporation (www.ziglar.com), founded by one of the greatest communicators of the twentieth century, has a number of programs designed to train people to become great sales representatives, speakers, and leaders. Whether you want to improve your presentation skills or simply reach your greatest potential in your personal or professional life, the Ziglar Corporation can help. They have helped me grow exponentially in many areas of my professional career as a communicator.

Finally, Bradley Communications (http://www.steveharrison.com), led by Steve Harrison, is a wonderful organization to help entrepreneurs market, lead, and present their messages in a highly effective and persuasive manner. They have coached thousands of authors, salespeople, entrepreneurs, and public speakers. They have helped authors like Robert Kiyosaki and Jack Hanfield, both *New York Times* best-selling authors.

In the preceding pages, we talked about the essence of a great communicator. In short, we talked about the who. The next chapter lays out the skills that great communicators use to lead people to transformational decisions—the how.

Questions for discussion or personal reflection:

1. How is your internal dialogue affecting the way you feel about yourself and what you're presenting? Are you confident about who you are and the solutions you offer? What are some of the areas where you feel weak or inadequate?

2. How do you truly feel about what you sell, present, or offer? Do you transfer your feelings with ease? If not, what is holding you back?

3. Can you see the invisible when you tell a story or communicate with others? Think about three of the most meaningful stories you've lived. Why are they so important to you?

4. In what ways can you become more effective in the art of communication? In your opinion, who is one of the best communicators you've heard? Why do you feel he or she is so effective?

5. What's the most important thing you've learned in this chapter?

Chapter 4

How to
Communicate Powerfully

No matter the profession, career, or position, powerful communicators have increased influence and income. Think about it. When an athlete writes and speaks well like Joe Montana, he or she can make hundreds of thousands of dollars through speaking engagements or book sales. The same is true of doctors like Dr. Oz, lawyers like Bill Handel, and politicians like Bill Clinton. This is especially true of salespeople like Zig Ziglar and celebrities like Oprah Winfrey. It's even true of ministers like Billy Graham and T. D. Jakes. Powerful communicators in any field are more effective, earn more money, and develop a larger following.

Every one of the examples of powerful communicators I've mentioned use persuasion to move people toward transformational decisions. Leadership is important, but it's not enough. It lays the foundation. But if you truly want to reach your greatest potential in any profession, you must learn the how-tos of powerful communication.

So what makes a powerful communicator? What separates great communicators from mediocre ones? There are seven skills that all great communicators develop that allow them to lead people toward transformational decisions. They are the how-tos of powerful communication. The first is *seeing the need*.

1. Seeing the Need

Mr. Smith crossed his arms and exclaimed, "I don't like the price, and I don't like the color!" Then he asked, "Why does it cost so much money?" David was a good sales representative, but what made him good wasn't smooth talk or slick presentations. He possessed neither of these qualities. Instead, he had a much more important gift. He could read his customers. Discerning the difference between a smokescreen and a legitimate concern, he discovered what his customers needed.

Three weeks earlier, Mr. Smith made a subtle comment during their first conversation. He said, "David, my grandchildren are important to me. I want to leave them a healthy business." That comment made all the difference during David's final presentation.

David believed that Mr. Smith would eventually buy the product, because he understood what he needed. The explosive objection didn't detour or intimidate him. Instead, he took a deep breath, and looked Mr. Smith in the eye. "Let me tell you why I think this is the best solution for what you are trying to accomplish," he said.

As he pulled out his tablet with a picture of the mockup sign he wanted to sell to his customer, he continued, "People don't give money to small businesses in exchange for a service. They give their money to people. When people buy from you, they believe you are doing the work for them. They enter into a business agreement, because they trust you. Your company, Mr. Smith, is only as trustworthy as you are. That's why your face needs to be on the sign. Your face has to be part of the branding of your company."

David pointed to the computer-generated image of a sign

with Mr. Smith's face prominently displayed on it. "The color matches the branding campaign we're proposing. My research indicates that we need a sign this size so that people can easily identify you. That costs money, Mr. Smith, but it's money well spent. If we stick to this campaign, your business will be profitable for years for your family members who take over."

David didn't blink or turn away. He looked steadily at Mr. Smith, gently pressed his lips together, and smiled assuredly. Mr. Smith looked down, and after a long and pensive pause said, "How long will it take to install?"

"If I have your approval today," David confidently said, "it will take ten days to make, and you should see some increase in revenue before the end of the first quarter."

Mr. Smith needed a sign and a comprehensive marketing plan, but he wanted to save money. More than anything, he wanted to grow his business and leave his grandchildren a healthy entity. David read his client in spite of the initial rejection, and that enabled him to clearly present the best solution.

Persuasive communicators know that their audience is comprised of four different types of people. The first group wants to know the bottom line and wants you to have proven results. This group wants you to get to the point. The second group wants to see enthusiasm and passion. This group is more sociable and wants to develop a relationship with you. The third group wants to feel that you have empathy and the ability to guide them to the solution they need. Finally, the fourth group wants to hear a logical presentation with stats, guarantees, and proof that the solution is the right one for them. They don't want to be bogged down by an emotional appeal.

For group one, **"Get to the point,"** this book should only be about eight pages long. Plus, they'll want me to have copies in the back of my car, or they'll want to download it immediately. Group two, **"Show me some passion,"** would rather talk about the content of this work in an informal gathering, perhaps over lunch. The third group, **"Let me know you care,"** would like me to extend the book another 150 pages and take all the necessary time to clearly demonstrate that I have the right solution for them. But before they buy the book, they want time to think about their purchase. **"Just stick to the facts,"** the final group, would like to see me quote more scholars and show more research to prove that I have done all my homework.

Among the people in the four groups are some who coexist in two groups. For example, some people are sociable and want people to get to the point. Others want you to show you've done your research and be passionate about your topic. Of course, we all possess some of the characteristics in each area, but we tend to be stronger in one or two.

For that reason I use a balance of narrative and informational content in my writing, presenting, and speaking. Narrative content includes stories, illustrations, jokes, and pictorial and visual language. Stories connect well with groups one, two and three. Stats, logic, and numerical graphs connect well with groups one, three, and four. Informational content includes stats, logic, and numerical graphs. If I can put together a written or verbal presentation that has both of these elements, there will be something for everyone. So the key to becoming a powerful communicator is having a decent balance of each of the two qualities (narrative and informational) to keep your audience engaged.

In order to communicate with a wide variety of people in one-on-one meetings, small business presentations, classrooms, and large arenas, keep several things in mind. Be direct, concise, and to the point. Don't overwhelm people with information, but allow them to see that additional information is available if they need it. Be sociable, passionate, and excited. Anticipate their questions before they ask them, and make sure your pace isn't too fast. I tell those I coach to use fewer words, but choose words that say more. This is true if you're a presenter, speaker, or writer. It will allow you to communicate more in less time without feeling rushed. Finally, do your homework, show your proof, and display some structure for those who need it.

2. Understanding Desire

"What can I say to these people? Do I really have anything to offer them?" Emily was terrified of making a presentation to the board. "Why my boss asked me to lead on this project is beyond me," she said. "I hate speaking. I hate selling. I hate standing up in front of groups!"

I asked her, "How many people will be in the room?"

"Nine," she replied.

Emily asked me to help her put together a presentation. When I think about her mental state at the time, I think she wanted an easy way out of the task. I assured her that no one dies from making presentations, and if she could get a broader perspective, she would do a great job and might even enjoy herself in the process. "I'll be lucky if I survive," she grumbled.

I asked her, "Tell me, what do the decision makers want out of the meeting?"

She said, "I have no idea."

"Well, there's your problem," I said. "If you knew what they wanted, wouldn't you give it to them?

"Of course I would," she replied.

"If you were certain you had exactly what they wanted, I bet you'd feel much more confident."

She said, "Yeah, that's easy to say, but how do you discover what people want?" As we will discover in this section, the simplest way is to ask them.

I suggested that Emily send an e-mail to each person who was going to be in the room during her presentation. "Send them three simple questions. Once they answer, you'll have fifty percent of your research done. Then compose a presentation that clearly shows how you can help them reach their objectives." At first, she seemed skeptical, but eventually agreed.

Then I told her, "Don't just send the e-mail and ask them to answer the questions. Preface your questions with the following context, 'I am looking forward to serving you the best I can, but I have a sense that you are facing some significant challenges. In order to prepare for our time together, I would like to get a broader perspective by asking you three basic questions. Please take your time and expound as much as you wish on each of the following questions.'"

I wrote out these three questions on a sheet of paper and slid it across the table:

1. What is the single greatest frustration you face in your business today?
2. If you could wave a wand and make something wonderful happen in your company, what would you want to happen and why?
3. What's the most important thing you want to be remembered for in your organization?

The answer to the first question tells us what keeps people up at night. It's the one thing that steals their peace. If you find out what gnaws at people and present a solution, you'll give your clients one of the most important gifts, peace of mind. At least, you'll be able to move them in that direction.

The answer to the second question concerning a magic wand tells us about their dreams, objectives, and goals. It tells us where people want to go and what they want to do. If you can help people reach their goals, you become more than a salesperson or a consultant or a company representative, you become an ally. You become a team member. You move from sitting on the opposite side of the table to their side. Now, you're working together.

The answer to the third question, how you want to be remembered, reveals the reputation people want to build and the legacy they want to leave behind. Believe me, no sane individual wants to be remembered for destroying his or her organization. People want to have a decent legacy, and when you help them move toward that end, you are helping them make transformational decisions. All three of these questions are designed to help the communicator discover what people truly want.

Emily wrote the e-mail and sent it to the participants. To her surprise, they all responded at length. They offered several paragraphs of emotional expression and priceless information. She called me and said, "You won't believe what they said. I have so much information about what they want to accomplish that I can provide several solutions." Soon Emily's fear dissipated. She became emboldened and enthusiastic about the challenge and put together a first-rate presentation. As they walked out of the conference room that afternoon, each expressed heartfelt gratitude for Emily's presentation. Emily had a grin so wide she could have eaten a banana sideways.

Instead of asking What can I say to these people? or Do I really have anything to offer them? ask yourself how you can discover what your audience truly wants. Before you speak, make a presentation, or write a proposal, research your audience's aspirations, needs, and wants.

Imagine how powerful your presentation will be if you know what keeps your audience up at night or if you clearly understand their biggest frustrations. Discover their greatest fears. Find out what they would do if they could snap their fingers and make three specific things happen immediately. Ask them, "If you could do anything and know you wouldn't fail, what would you do?"

Having the answers to these inquiries will make you a powerful communicator. After all, knowledge is power, and it helps you provide solutions to people who are frustrated, stuck, and want to move forward. If you desire to help people move toward transformational decisions, then you need to know what motivates them and what they want.

I am convinced that people reluctantly buy what they need, but they enthusiastically buy what they want. Have you ever seen people line up to buy broccoli or cauliflower? Probably not. People need vegetables, but they don't go out of their way to buy them. Instead, they line up after Thanksgiving dinner outside a superstore to buy a large screen television or some other gadget. They find the money to buy what they want to buy. They find the time to do what they want to do. They find a way to go where they want to go. So discover what your audience truly wants by doing your homework ahead of time and finding the answers to some of the inquiries mentioned above.

3. Reading Your Audience

I was about to travel to a speaking engagement in a small community three hours north of Minneapolis. As I headed out the door my father-in-law stopped me. "Jason, there's one thing you need to know about the people in that coal mining town," he said. "They're not easy to read." He went on, "They may or may not laugh at your jokes. They probably won't give you a standing ovation or even clap when you're finished, but you can learn to read them by watching their eyes."

After I was introduced to speak, I began my presentation. I am eternally grateful that my father-in-law shared his insight about the body language of my audience. They spoke English, as do I. They had blue eyes, like mine. They were all born and raised in the United States. But when I started to speak, I felt I was speaking to an indigenous tribe in the Amazon jungle. They were educated and civilized, but they looked at me as if they were watching a freshly painted wall dry. They were not expressive, and no one nodded in agreement with any of my points. However, their eyes indicated they were with me. When I moved from left to right, they followed me across the stage. When I paused, they didn't flinch. No one looked at his or her phone or watch, or got up to go to the restroom.

During a portion of the presentation covering some research, I could tell that a few people were developing heavy eyelids. So I quickly introduced a story, which regained their attention and strengthened my connection with them. After my address was finished, I thanked them for their attention and wished them the best. The host came forward and said in a dispassionate manner, "I don't know about you folks, but that presentation thrilled me." His body language didn't match his words, but down deep inside, he was appreciative. When the crowd was dismissed, many of them passed by my table, shook my hand, and personally thanked me for my participation. Up to that moment, I thought I simply survived my speech, when in fact people sincerely enjoyed it.

One of the most powerful communication skills you can develop is reading your audience during the presentation. Picking up on the subtleties such as body language, eye contact, and responsiveness will tell you if you need to shift gears, change directions, or quickly edit your material. Audiences and clients will warn you before they completely disconnect from your presentation. Watch for more than one person nodding off. Look for more than one person who constantly stares at their smart phone. Notice if more than one person is sitting with arms crossed or consistently whispering something in their neighbor's ear. Why do I say more than one person? Because in every audience or large sales presentation, someone will nod off. The same is true of those who tinker with their phones or look at their watches. There's one in every crowd. Don't panic if just one person seems disinterested in what you have to say.

But if you see several audience members looking distracted, then you need to pay attention. If their eyes are getting glassy, make a quick transition to something more compelling to them. This is what I call editing on the spot. It separates great speakers from mediocre ones. Presenters and speakers who do not understand this important skill run the risk of losing their audience or something worse. They might push them away from transformational decisions to total apathy.

Too many times, I've seen communicators sticking to a script that no one cares about. Instead of reading the cues given by their clients or audience, they work through their material as if they are driving on a long dirt road in the desert. In the meantime, the audience is asking, "Are we there yet?"

Clients should never have to suffer through a presentation. Audience members shouldn't be glancing at their smart phones or tablets, wondering when the boredom will finally end. Why make things more difficult on yourself? Instead, learn the power of editing during your presentation. Whether you are communicating to five or five thousand, the following techniques will help turn things around quickly in any presentation.

If you are unsure whether your audience is with you, ask them an interesting question about the topic of your presentation. For example, "How many of you would like to . . . ?" or, "Would any of you like to guess what the number one way is to . . . ?"

Another way you can turn the tide is to pause. Few communicators master the art of the pause. Great communicators keep people on the edge of their seats by simply taking a few seconds to say, "One of the most powerful things I've ever learned was . . . ." Then pause for a moment without a word before you finish your sentence. Be purposeful. Know what you are going to say. Don't look confused or lost. Look natural, convincing, and assured.

Over the years, one technique I have found to be effective is an occasional moment when I whisper an important point or sentence. It causes people to turn their heads slightly, because they want to hear what seems to be secretive. There's a fine balance, though. You must whisper loud enough so that everyone can hear but be faint enough to cause your audience to respond by intentionally focusing on your words. If you achieve that balance, your presentation will take on a whole new dynamic.

As mentioned earlier in this book, the most effective way to connect with an audience is to tell them a story. In almost every case, a well-applied story will redeem what seems to be a lost presentation. You will see a transformation of your audience when you take them on a narrative journey. Nothing engages an audience quicker than a good story.

4. Valuing Introversion

"I wouldn't be good at sales. I'm too shy, and I hate rejection." Those were the words of Stephanie, a twenty-three-year-old college dropout.

"Shyness has nothing to do with it," I assured her. "Introverts make great communicators and great salespeople."

"How's that?" she asked in disbelief.

"They have a gift that extroverts usually lack. They are good observers because they generally don't talk too much."

"What does that have to do with sales?" Stephanie asked.

"Powerful communicators have good content. Their delivery isn't just about a good performance. Great communicators have something worth saying. Take the time to find out what your customers need and figure out a way to solve their problem. Then allow your convictions to come out. I promise with time you'll become a sales representative."

"What do you mean by 'allow your convictions to come out'?" she asked.

I knew that if she could grasp that concept, she would become highly successful. So I went on to explain, "Introverts take in and process a ton of information because they listen and watch. But then their beliefs about something become convictions. Convictions are strong feelings that drive us to action. They help us overcome barriers, shyness, or setbacks, to do what we believe is right. So when you allow your convictions to come out, you convey with confidence that you have the right course of action. You will seem genuine and sincere. Nothing is more crucial in communication than sincerity and genuineness."

The following Monday, Stephanie applied for an associate sales position at a Fortune 500 company. She was hired and within a year she had her own territory in the Midwest. Twelve months later, she became the top representative in her office. The following year, she became the number one sales representative in her district. After a decade, she became one of the youngest regional vice-presidents in the organization. Today, she travels around the world training sales representatives and marketers to listen to the needs of their customers.

This story illustrates an important point. Although being an introvert doesn't qualify you to be a great communicator, sales representative, leader, actor, or teacher, neither does being an extrovert. Introverts have an advantage that allows them to see into the hearts of their audience. Because of their listening skills and insights, they can come up with a plan that strategically meets the needs of those they aim to help.

If you are an extrovert who likes to talk, develop the ability to close your mouth and open your ears. Move off the stage, and give your customers, constituents, and clients the spotlight. Let them reveal their strengths, weaknesses, dreams, and aspirations. Encourage them to share their victories and accomplishments as well as their defeats and disappointments. You will discover that people love to talk about themselves if given the chance.

5. Focusing on One

My college professor started the class by telling a story. He told us about a little girl who overcame a significant barrier in order to live a fruitful and significant life. It was one of those stories you never forget. When he finished, he said, "You see, friend, if she can overcome her barrier, you can too." Then he began his lecture.

The first thing I noticed about his story was that it was about one person, not fifty. People don't identify with crowds. They identify with a person. Customers identify with a customer. Passengers identify with a passenger. Parents identify with a parent. Students identify with a student, and all of us identify with a lonely soul who wants to find his or her true love. We enjoy a story about someone who moves from desperate poverty to financial stability. Why is that?

We tend to see ourselves in the characters of stories, and when there are too many characters, it is difficult to see how they develop. When there is no character development, there is no connection between the illustration and listener or reader. Great communicators understand that powerful illustrations deal with a main character who goes through trials and tribulations before reaching her goal, victory, or resolution. When you share a story with an audience, make a sales presentation, write an op-ed, or share something significant with a client, don't forget to emphasize how one person's life changed.

The second interesting thing the professor did was use the word friend. He didn't sound like he was speaking to a crowd of a hundred university students. He was speaking to one hundred individuals, one at a time. That is what great communicators do. They speak about one person and they speak to one person. They write about one person and they write to one person. The radio talk show host talks to one person (the listener) in the same way a newscaster speaks to one person (the viewer).

During the commercial break of my first radio interview, my host said, "Don't say, 'I want to say hi to all the listeners.' Instead, speak to one person. The audience may be a million, but they are one million individuals. They want to feel that you are talking directly to them." What great advice. The same is true in radio, television, and speaking to small groups or arenas with tens of thousands of people. Whenever I make a presentation, I speak to one person at a time.

How can you speak to one person at a time in large audience? Look directly at one individual and talk to that person. After you look at her for two or three seconds, move on to another person and talk to that person for a second or two. Continue to do that throughout your total presentation, and cover the entire room with good eye contact. Don't just look at the person and talk. Really communicate with each person. Make each person feel that you are engaged with him or her in a transformational conversation.

Whether they tell stories about one individual or speak to individuals in a crowd, great communicators harness the power of the one and use it to their advantage.

6. Using Vocal Dynamics

The crowd looked exhausted. It was the last morning of a three-day seminar. The night before, the session ended at one o'clock in the morning. Tom's sales presentation would be the final one of the convention. He knew that if his presentation wasn't interesting, he would lose the audience in minutes.

Moments before Tom was introduced to speak, he approached the producer and asked permission to step off the stage during his presentation and walk among the crowd. The

Power To Persuade

producer agreed.

The host introduced Tom and gave him the microphone. He placed his notes on the podium, looked at the audience for a moment and started by saying, "Today could be the most important day of your life." Then Tom proceeded to tell a story as he walked off the stage. He walked slowly but with a specific destination in mind. He headed to the camera platform situated in the middle of the crowd. Those in the first twenty rows were forced to turn ninety degrees in order to see him. He stood on the platform just behind the camera operators who were unable to turn their cameras around. He stood there for two minutes and slowly made his way back to the stage as he wrapped up the story.

He slowed his presentation. Then he increased his velocity. He lowered his voice, then raised it. When it was appropriate, he paused, stared at the crowd, and waited an extra second or two before continuing. He never changed his content. He didn't change his purpose. He never altered his close. He simply changed his delivery.

Great communicators have presence. They have an incredible ability to project through the first row all the way to the person sitting in the last seat in the venue. Whether it's Luis Miguel, Ronald Reagan, Michael Jackson, Anthony Robbins, or C. S. Lewis, effective communicators develop the skill to make every observer, listener, or reader feel that he or she is part of the presentation. How do you become a dynamic speaker? Here are a few things to consider.

First, powerful communicators know that monotone is monotone, even when you are screaming. If you do not vary your voice in tone, pitch, and volume, you sound monotonous, plain, and uninteresting. At the right moment, lower your voice, then raise your voice. Sound excited, thrilled, convinced, and thoughtful. Be enthusiastic, passionate, and considerate. There are times when a great speaker will sound sad, moved, and disillusioned. He or she may even cry. Whatever you do, don't sound robotic or zombie-like. Sound interesting.

Second, powerful communicators move during their presentations or speeches. And they move with purpose. They don't pace back and forth across the stage nervously without thinking. Instead, they move to strategic locations on the stage, in an office, or living room. They do so with a specific reason in mind, keeping everyone engaged in the presentation.

Third, dynamic presenters vary the speed of their delivery. They say more with fewer words. They slow down when they want to emphasize and speed up when the audience can fill in the blanks. This allows them to spend time on the areas they want to emphasize and move quickly through the areas that are not as vital.

Fourth, powerful communicators don't simply fill the airwaves with lots of words. If they want something to sink in, they give it time to do so. They know how to pause and not look confused. When they pause, they look into the eyes of their audience and find their next statement there. The pause creates a dynamic moment that brings the audience to the edge of their seats.

7. Keeping it Simple

I have never seen such a complex presentation in my life, I thought. I sat in the audience completely confused. The speaker presented seventy-five different points spread across forty different PowerPoint slides. What was the topic? Five simple principles to start a successful business.

The PowerPoint slides looked sharp. The speaker was gracious and seemed knowledgeable. When he finished, I wasn't quite sure what to think. At first, I thought perhaps I was disengaged because I was tired. But when I looked around, I saw many people sending e-mails, updating their Facebook pages, or tweeting their followers. The comments in the hallway afterward were not gracious. I heard, "That guy is the cure for insomnia," and, "Remind me never to take that seminar again." The speaker's problem wasn't a lack of knowledge. It wasn't a lack of preparation or passion for his topic. He failed to execute one of the most important principles of communication, *making the complex simple*.

The one thing great communicators do better than most is make complex concepts understandable to everyone. Socrates said, "True wisdom comes to each of us when we realize how little we understand about life, ourselves, and the world around us." Abraham Lincoln's Gettysburg Address contains only 278 words. Of those words, 210 have only one syllable. Jesus made the concept of eternal life understandable to everyone, especially the poor in spirit.

Use your words as a strategic tool to sculpt an effective presentation, a dynamic story, and a life-changing close. Make every word count for something. If a word doesn't work, exchange it for a more effective one. Make every sentence a steppingstone that leads your customers, clients, or audience to transformational decisions. When you communicate in the simplest way you can, you lay the groundwork to becoming the powerful communicator you were born to be.

Practical Steps to Effective Communication

Whenever you have a presentation, speech, or sales call to make, arrive early and take a look at the setting. When possible, explore the venue. From different vantage points, imagine yourself speaking to a full house. Visualize your audience's reaction. Anticipate their objections. Feel their struggles, their pain, their aspirations, their hopes, and dreams. Then purpose in your heart to help them as best as you can.

Whether you use props, skits, PowerPoint slides, or video in your presentation is entirely up to you. Just make sure that you are the driving force behind these aids. Do not allow these elements to control your presentation. Make sure you have the freedom to edit your presentation, in case you need to adjust your content or approach.

When you present, be compelling, entertaining, life-changing, logical, professional, humble, and in alignment with your golden thread. Mention your spouse, your family, your upbringing, and your desire to help your audience. Why are these things so important? Nothing gives a speaker greater credibility than a supportive family. Nothing says "I'm worth listening to" more than when you are professional, authoritative, and in alignment with your golden thread. Nothing will connect you with your customers, clients, and audience faster than being human.

The following outline is a basic and effective structure to help you put together your presentation.

Introduction—Break the ice and share why you are credible
- Communicate a clear idea of what you're going to talk about and why it's crucial
- State the problem and the people it affects
- Ask the audience if they have faced similar issues
- Use a transitional statement and first close, which finalizes the lesson or proposed offer.

State your first point
- Use stats, numbers, evidence, and supporting info
- Tell a story or share an illustration to reinforce your first point
- Repeat the first point
- Transition to the second point and second close

State your second point
- Use stats, numbers, evidence, and supporting info
- Tell a story or share an illustration to reinforce the second point
- Repeat the second point
- Transition to the third point and third close

State your third point
- Use stats, numbers, evidence, and supporting info
- Tell a story or share an illustration to reinforce the third point
- Repeat the third point
- Give a one-sentence summary of each point

Conclusion and final close

Let me close this chapter by stating a most important lesson. Powerful communication, great selling, and effective leadership are not innate traits. They are skills that can be taught and learned. I am convinced that if you put into practice these principles, you will develop the skills to become a highly persuasive communicator.

Questions for discussion or personal reflection:

1. Why is distinguishing the difference between what your customers want and what they need so important? Which one is more powerful? Why? What are some of the best questions you've ever asked your customers or clients? How did those questions create opportunities for you?

2. What can you do to prevent people from mentally checking out of your presentations? Name some examples of how to keep them engaged.

3. Why do introverts have an advantage in sales, acting, writing, and speaking?

4. Why is simplification so important in communication? What are some practical ways you can make your presentations, writing, or speaking more concrete and relatable?

5. What's the most important thing you've learned in this chapter?

Section III

Persuasive Solutions

Chapter 5

Breaking Your Glass Ceiling

Do you dream of reaching the top of your profession or becoming the best in your field? If so, what's holding you back? Seriously, do you want to change the world with your product or idea, lead your organization, make millions, or simply elevate your family to a whole new standard of living? What is preventing you? Is it a glass ceiling or another form of prejudice or discrimination? Might it be a boss who constantly misreads you? Is it a lack of money, education, or resources? Maybe you haven't gotten the break you deserve.

Nido Qubein, a successful businessman and award-winning motivational speaker who is himself an immigrant, said, "Immigrants to America are four times as likely to become millionaires as born Americans."[1] What is it that empowers them to break the barriers and shatter the glass ceiling? First of all, they don't believe the lie that *it can't be done*. By the time they've figured out that America has problems, it's too late. They've already discovered the road to financial success.

Second, they've moved thousands of miles, dealt with family uprooting, faced culture shock, and overcome significant language barriers. If they can endure such adversities, what would prevent them from working eighty hours a week and living as paupers to forge a successful future for their families?

Whether you are an immigrant, female, or minority, most likely you've had to deal with a glass ceiling or other barrier to advancement in your profession. The truth is, regardless of your race, nationality, gender, age, or socioeconomic status, you may feel there is some hindrance to your success. So which is worse, a perceived obstacle or an actual one? The illusion of a barrier can be as discouraging as a real one. Prejudice and discrimination are debilitating whether they are real or imagined.

Powerful persuaders move beyond their barriers and impediments to reach their greatest potential. That is my desire for you. The goal of this chapter is to give you four incredible insights to help you overcome the obstacles that prevent you from moving forward and climbing upward. The first insight is strengthening and energizing your greatest asset.

1. Strengthening Your Greatest Asset

My wife and I were heading toward the convention center in downtown Milwaukee when our hosts, Teodoro and Noemi Esquivel, shared something that truly moved me. They are members of Signature Equipovision, a large organization made up of entrepreneurs. A couple of years earlier their president, Juan Ruelas, addressed a large group of representatives and leaders and said, "Please don't tell me you came to this country to watch television!" He went on to say, "Why in the world would you travel so far, put your family through such adversity, and take such a huge risk just to sit on your couch and watch television?"

As my hosts told me what it was like to hear those words as an immigrant from an immigrant, I thought to myself, *that phrase really nails it!* Why do so many people sit around and waste time when they aspire to accomplish great things? Why do they let thousands of hours slip by while other influences control their destiny? Juan's comments are true for anyone (not just immigrants) who allows his or her life to be governed by mindless entertainment. When you don't take charge and carve out your own destiny, someone or something else will.

This section focuses on your greatest asset, which is not a rich uncle or a mother who loves you. It's not your spouse or the country in which you live. It's the mind that rests between your ears. You were beautifully and wonderfully created to reach new heights and discover wonderful frontiers. You, my friend, were destined for greatness and designed to live life fully. I do not believe that you are here on earth by chance or to simply survive. My deepest conviction is that the purpose for your life is to live. And if there is anything I want this book to help you do, it is to help you live an exceptional life.

As we have noted, one of the most effective ways to live life is to stay in harmony with your golden thread. So how can you fulfill your golden thread and live out your purpose if you do not have the emotional energy to do so? If you're not motivated and can't find the energy to move forward, how will you break the glass ceiling above your head, the concrete barrier in your path, or the bars of prejudice that keep you from accomplishing your dreams? One of the reasons people sit on the couch and let life pass them by is they lack the emotional energy to get up and move in the right direction.

If you are going to break down the barrier, you first need to raise your level of emotional energy that fuels your mind to take action. You may be thinking, *What in the world does this have to do with persuasive solutions?* It has everything to do with them. Without energy, you can't solve problems, be proactive, or motivate others. Without emotional energy, you won't be able to get off the couch.

That's why I tell everyone I coach to start an exercise regimen.

Obviously, you need to consult a physician before you embark upon anything that affects your health. Nevertheless, almost every medical doctor, internist, neurologist, psychiatrist, or psychologist will say that the key to good mental and emotional health is exercise. It builds stamina, longevity, and strength. Some people argue that you need emotional energy in order to exercise. This is true. However, you won't get motivated to exercise until you start exercising. Once you start, you get the energy to exercise more. Eventually, you will find the energy required to continue exercising regularly.

The same is true regarding what you put into your body. Eating right makes a world of difference in your emotional strength as well. At first, eating right requires emotional energy, but after a while you receive much more energy from good eating habits than what is required to maintain those habits. I cannot emphasize this enough. You cannot reach your greatest potential if you carry too much weight or have uncontrolled sugar levels, high blood pressure, or a lack of stamina. So take care of your greatest asset—you. You will need energy to break whatever barrier you face or the glass ceiling that blocks you.

2. Capitalizing on Your Leverage

Jennifer was the first to discover that the company she and her husband, John, owned had been suspended by the state of California because of a single document the accountant failed to file with their tax return. "I couldn't sleep last night so I decided to catch up on some paperwork," she said. "That's when I noticed that according to the website of the Secretary of State of California because there is another corporation with the same name as ours, our business license has been suspended."

"What!?" John exclaimed in disbelief. "How in the world did that happen?"

"I have no idea," she replied, "but I'll call the lawyer."

The couple owned a small auto detailing service. Their biggest competitor was an international corporation who had locations in ten states and two other countries. Since their company names were identical except for one word, I am giving them fictitious names. Let's say that the larger company was called Power Detailing International. The smaller company was called Power Detailing, Inc.

Jennifer called the attorney, and he said, "Are you sitting down?"

"Why?" she asked.

"Remember the delay in filing your taxes two and half years ago? Apparently, your status was suspended temporarily and after a certain amount of time another entity grabbed the name of your corporation."

"Wait a minute! Are you saying we no longer can use our name?"

"That's correct," replied the attorney.

"Who took the name?"

"According to the Secretary of State's website it's Power Detailing International."

John grabbed the phone and asked the attorney, "Tell me, what names are available that are similar to ours? Perhaps one is available that will work well for us."

The attorney looked over the Secretary of State's website, and said, "Wait a minute. This can't be."

"What is it?" John asked.

"Unless I'm seeing this wrong, Power Detailing International is suspended."

"Say that again," John uttered with a tinge of disbelief.

"According to the website, *Power Detailing International* is available. Apparently the company didn't file their tax returns in time in California. In essence, the same thing that happened to you has happened to them. Let me call the Secretary of State's office to confirm this." Pausing for a moment, he asked one final question. "Before I call, do you want me to secure that name if it's available?"

John responded with an unequivocal yes.

Twenty minutes later the lawyer called John with the news. "You are now the proud owner of the corporate name Power Detailing International." John waited a week before he made a call to the larger company.

The receptionist said, "Power Detailing International, how may I direct your call?"

"May I please speak to Mr. Smith?" John said.

"Who may I ask is calling?" the receptionist replied.

"My name is John Palmer. I own Power Detailing International."

"Excuse me? Did you say that you own this company?"

"No, I do not own your company. I own my company whose legal name is Power Detailing International."

Somewhat perplexed, the receptionist replied, "Uh, please hold."

Within ten seconds, John was speaking to Mr. Smith, the CEO of the corporation. "This is Mr. Smith. Can I help you?"

John replied, "Perhaps I can help you. I would like my corporate name back."

"What do you mean?" the CEO asked.

John said, "For years, my wife and I had the corporate name Power Detailing, Inc. We've always filed our tax returns on time, but one year the state apparently didn't receive our paperwork and suspended our status. By the time we figured out what happened, you swooped in and took our name."

"Well, my dear boy, that's what happens in business," Mr. Smith replied. "Besides, you're a small business, and we have offices throughout the United States and in several countries around the world. I don't have time to deal with your petty inquiry."

"That may be true," John replied. "But you are an international corporation, and now I control your original name. I just registered my corporate name *Power Detailing International* with the State of California, and guess what? I own the name!"

The CEO responded, "That's impossible!"

"Check the Secretary of State's website," John said. "Whether I do international business or not, everyone is going to think that I am you."

On the other end of the phone, John could hear the sound of fingers frantically typing on a keyboard followed by Mr. Smith softly whispering the words on his computer screen. Finally, there was a long sigh. "Can I call you back?"

John slowly and confidently said, "Take all the time you want."

Mr. Smith called his CFO into his office. "Have we filed all of our tax returns over the last five years?"

The CFO replied, "Yes, but our return from two years ago has had some discrepancies, and to be transparent, I've put the matter on the backburner to deal with our intention to refinance some of our capital debt."

Mr. Smith asked, "Are we in good shape with the state or not?" The CFO replied, "I believe so, but let me check," pulling

Power To Persuade

out his laptop and looking over the correspondence between the company and the government. "Well, it seems as though the state is threatening to suspend our status. Their last correspondence dated six months ago says that if we don't respond within thirty days, our status will be suspended. But they always say that. I wouldn't worry about it."

Mr. Smith clenched his jaw and shut his eyes. After a moment of silence, he reluctantly admitted, "We've lost our name! Another company has already stepped in, because we 'put it on the backburner'. Please leave. I need to make a phone call."

Mr. Smith called John and humbly asked, "What do you want?"

John responded, "I told you. I want our name back. If you don't give it back, I'm going to keep *Power Detailing International* until I die. Then I'll pass it on to my kids and grandchildren. Everyone will continue to think that my company is really yours."

A defeated Mr. Smith somberly said, "Fine. I'll have my lawyer contact yours."

Within a week, John had his original name restored.

This illustration is based upon a true story. I've changed many of the aspects in order to maintain the privacy of both organizations and the individuals involved. In the end, John wound up with what he needed, and Mr. Smith learned a valuable lesson as well.

John discovered his points of leverage in negotiating. He learned that if you want something, you must have the power to negotiate something. You must have power over something that the other entity wants. You must have leverage.

David, the ancient Israelite boy, used his leverage as a rock-slinging sharpshooter to conquer Goliath, a nine-foot giant. Rosa Parks used her leverage as a citizen bus rider to confront racial discrimination in 1955. The Allied Forces used their leverage as a unified army to eradicate the spread of Hitler's tyranny. Mahatma Gandhi used his leverage as a moral leader in opposition to British rule in India by pursuing a policy of nonviolent disobedience.

Leverage is simply the point from which you push off in order to overcome the resistance that is pushing against you. So stand on a solid foundation, one that you know you dominate. People who break barriers and shatter glass ceilings know where to place their feet and hands in order to push through that which holds them back. They know where their leverage is.

I want to emphasize that it is not how much leverage you have but what you do with it that counts. David didn't use a sword, a bow, or a private army to kill Goliath. He used one smooth stone and a sling. Rosa Parks didn't slap the bus driver or shove anyone; she simply sat down. Those who discover persuasive solutions know how to use what is at their disposal. And if they don't have what they need, they find the most efficient way to get it.

After you finish reading this chapter, make a list of the areas where you have leverage. Identify your strengths. What do you know? Are you bilingual or have a formal education? Are you a quick learner? What can you do? Do you have a strong work ethic? Who do you know? Do you have a list of resourceful contacts willing to help you in a strategic situation? In all of this, know what you dominate.

3. Becoming a First-rate Negotiator

I thought I knew how to sell. I thought I knew how to buy. I thought I knew how to negotiate, that is, until I went to Istanbul. My wife and I walked into the Grand Bazaar in the heart of the city that is the gateway between the European and Asian continents. It is one of the largest indoor markets in the world. Imagine hundreds upon hundreds of small stores selling every known article of clothing by every known designer (some authentic, others almost authentic). There was luggage, beautiful pottery, exquisite jewelry, gorgeous Turkish rugs, exotic spices, and just about every other imaginable thing to buy.

While my wife was busy in another store looking for souvenirs for our daughters, I stood in the middle of the corridor and tried to keep what little cash I had in my ever-thinning wallet protected. A young man with a cigarette dangling from the right corner of his mouth approached me. He quickly nodded upward and said in his notable Turkish accent, "Where you from?"

I replied, "From about seven thousand miles from here."

"Oh, you from Florida?"

"No."

"Which state are you from?" he persisted. "New York? Colorado? Washington?"

Growing tired of the conversation, I finally coughed up the information. "I'm from California."

"California? What a beautiful state."

Knowing that I'd better not encourage him, I simply nodded.

"Sir, if you live in such a beautiful state, let me show you something that would look fabulous in your California home. I have the best Turkish rugs in the Bazaar."

107

Breaking Your Glass Ceiling

"No, thank you." I said. "I'm really not interested."

"Don't you want to get your wife something beautiful to show her how much you love her?"

What a question. If I say no I sound like an inconsiderate husband. If I say yes I'm out a grand. So I said, "Of all the things I don't want to buy, a rug would be number one. I have no desire to buy one. I have no way of getting it home. I don't want to spend the money, and most importantly, I have two pets that will eat the thing in a matter of minutes upon its arrival."

After I fired off four fairly impressive objections, the man raised his eyebrows, and said with thickly accented English, "Good-a-luck, sir."

Ha, I thought to myself. I finally figured out how to get these vendors off my back. At least, so I thought. A young man who sold scarves listened to the whole conversation and noted everything I shared with the first vendor.

My wife continued to look over some trinkets in the shop to my left. My victory bought me a few seconds of time alone.

"So you're married with kids, huh?" the scarf vendor asked.

Well, I can't be rude, I thought. *I should probably acknowledge his question.* "Yes, that's correct."

"People in California have great taste and great style," he said. "Do you think your wife would be interested in one of my top quality scarves?"

"I really don't think so, but thank you," I said.

"It's cold outside, and your wife would appreciate something to protect her neck from the chill."

She had a scarf but wasn't wearing it at the time. Then I remembered that I needed a scarf. It was cold outside, and my ears nearly froze before walking into the Bazaar. However, I had no intention of buying in the Bazaar. Besides, everything on display in the man's shop was for women. I thought that I would use that as an excuse to not buy from him.

"I don't think she'd be interested. Besides you don't carry men's scarves, do you?"

"Do I have men's scarves?" the young man perked up. He stretched out his hand, and said, "My name is Murat, and I sell the very best men's scarves in Turkey."

Nuts! I thought to myself.

"Please step into my space, and I will show you neck scarves that will make your wife very happy."

I am the one who's supposed to be happy in this scenario, I thought. *Why is everyone trying to make her happy?* Deep down inside, I knew that if Cindee thought the scarf looked good, I would be much more likely to purchase one.

The vendor reached into a small square space located on the wall and pulled out a black scarf made of a very soft and fine material. He wrapped it around my neck and stood back and said with total confidence, "Now that looks great on you!"

Trying to sound disinterested, I responded, "I don't know. I guess it's okay. How much is it?"

"Three hundred dollars US."

"Three hundred dollars?" I gasped. "What's it made of?"

"The finest cashmere in the country," he confidently replied.

"Well, do you have anything in cotton?"

That was the question he was waiting for.

"Of course I do," he said, reaching into another cubbyhole. He began to wrap a gray colored scarf around my neck and said, "Let's try this one." He tied it in a special knot, took a step back, and said, "It's perfect."

At that moment, my wife walked into the small shop and said, "Oh, that's a beautiful scarf. You should get it."

Before I could ask, Murat, who knew how this negotiation would turn out said, "It's twenty-five dollars US." I breathed a sigh of relief and offered him twenty dollars. He paused a moment and said, "Normally, I wouldn't discount this piece of fine clothing, but for you I'll make an exception."

Murat understood something very important. We were in the Bazaar because we were buying things. That means we had money to spend. He also knew that if my wife thought I looked good in a scarf, I was much more likely to buy it. He noted that I wanted to get a good deal, stay warm, and look decent. But more than anything else, he wanted to make a profit. After all, he had a business to maintain and a family to feed. As Cindee and I exited the Bazaar with several bags of trinkets and clothes, I noticed another store selling scarfs. They had a scarf exactly like the one I bought ten minutes before. How much was it? Fifteen dollars.

This is a story about a twenty dollar negotiation, but the process of great negotiation is the same whether you're dealing with twenty dollars or $200 million. It's important that you give before you take. You must listen in order to understand and articulate in order to be understood. Whether you're working out the details of a treaty, the purchase of your next home, your work schedule, a promotion, or pay increase, the following steps will help you become a great negotiator.

First, *understand what the other person truly wants.* Sometimes, a sense of frustration causes emotions to cloud our ability to clearly discern what the core issues are. When one country enters into negotiations with another country, for example, it knows where its leverage is, what it wants, and what the other country wants. If they truly want the negotiations to succeed, they avoid asking questions that will derail the process.

POWER TO PERSUADE

Skilled negotiators give others a sense that they want what is best for all parties involved.

As you enter into negotiations, ask the right questions so that everyone with whom you're dealing feels that you genuinely want to help. Why is this so important? Because when you can help others acquire what they truly want, you move from being an adversary to an advisor. When they feel you are truly interested in helping them get what they want, they are much more likely to help you get what you want.

Second, *understand what is sacred to others*. The shopkeeper Murat understood that my wife's opinion was important whether I would admit it or not. He understood that I didn't want to spend too much money. He understood that people guard that which is important to them, and if threatened, they will take extreme measures to protect it. For some, it's money. For others, it's power. It could be a physical possession, a principle, a reputation, or avoiding humiliation.

Further, we all have buttons that when pushed cause reactions that are not favorable to the best outcome. So stay away from factors that are detrimental to the negotiation process. If it's not a hill worth dying on for you, then why bother mentioning it? Why risk derailing your mission? Sometimes keeping your mouth shut over a certain topic is the wisest thing you can do.

Third, *learn to analyze the concerns and motivations of others*. The number one problem for salespeople, entrepreneurs, and just about anyone involved in a negotiation is learning to listen. As a matter of fact, I would say that most are average listeners at best. People will tell you everything you need to know if you will keep quiet long enough to hear what they say or pick up on the subtleties they drop. Look at their body language. Watch their eye contact. Listen to their off-the-cuff remarks. If nothing else, be direct and ask them the following two questions: What's the one thing you want? And, Would you be interested in hearing how I can help you get it? When they give you their answer, the negotiation starts with this follow-up question: If I can give you A, would you be willing to offer me B in return?

Fourth, *be wise and strategic in the negotiating process.* Don't reveal everything you have in your arsenal at the beginning. Only divulge what you have at your disposal as it becomes necessary, and only offer what you can afford to live without. When you present something, make sure it is a satisfactory gesture. There's nothing worse than offering something that no one cares about. Otherwise, you run the risk of sounding oblivious to the other party's needs and desires.

4. What To Do in the Face of *No*

A few years ago, my publisher urged me to find several compelling endorsements for a new book that I had written, *Breaking the Barriers*. As you may have deduced by now, Zig Ziglar is one of my all-time heroes of sales, motivation, and persuasion. I knew that Mr. Ziglar was highly in demand, but I felt that his endorsement would give my book the credibility it deserved. I went to his website and asked the webmaster to pass along my request to Mr. Ziglar to consider endorsing my book.

The next morning, Mr. Ziglar's executive assistant, Laurie Magers, responded with the kindest, most professional "we respectfully decline" e-mail I've ever received. It started off with "Good morning, Jason." Then she diplomatically spent several paragraphs explaining to me that Mr. Ziglar's board had mandated that he read every manuscript cover to cover before issuing an endorsement and that because of his age (82) he no longer offered endorsements, simply because he was committed to completing several new books. Laurie had been Zig Ziglar's assistant for thirty-one years, and he was now struggling with some health issues that kept him from many of the pursuits he found enjoyable and beneficial over the years. She finished her e-mail with this statement: "Mr. Ziglar is always honored to be invited to comment on someone's new book, Jason, and we thank you for making this opportunity available to him." I was not only impressed by the fact that she responded but also with her kindness, integrity, and courteous attitude.

Given that she issued three strong reasons why Mr. Ziglar would not be able to issue an endorsement, I probably should have folded my tent and walked away. Something inside me, though, felt that Zig Ziglar, my sales coach, would have been disappointed if I gave up.

So the next day, I wrote Laurie back expressing my profound gratitude for her response. I told her that I was deeply impressed with her kind and professional spirit. "Zig is fortunate to have had you for thirty-one years," I said. Then I added, "Having said that, you know that Zig would be extremely disappointed in me if I didn't take the objection as a wonderful opportunity to clarify my understanding of his needs. So I want you to know that I have some good news and a gift."

I clarified that I did not need the blurb anytime soon. He could take up to seven months if necessary. Then I offered them a sincere no-strings-attached gift, something that I believed would be of great value to them.

I wrote, "Zig's inspirational messages have had such a profound impact on me that I would be glad to record a testimonial that he could use for any purposes he sees fit. As a matter of fact, regardless of whether he considers writing the endorsement or not, I offer this to him as a gift. I have a live daily radio program on Radio Nueva Vida, the largest Spanish nonprofit network in the United States with over 500,000 listeners. I would be glad to use my gifts to help him in any way I can."

The next day, Laurie responded, "You probably will not be surprised to learn that I was not surprised to hear from you again with 'Plan B'. It has been our forever policy to never say never, so in that context you may feel free to send your manuscript. The one thing I cannot do is promise or guarantee that Mr. Ziglar will 1) read it or 2) offer the requested endorsement." Then she gave me the address.

She ended her e-mail with this final statement: "P.S. We'd be grateful for and appreciate that testimonial. With it will you give us your permission to use it in any form of media, please? I can tell you it will be personally meaningful to Mr. Ziglar."

I responded with an unequivocal yes. Even if Mr. Ziglar wouldn't issue an endorsement, the fact that he would consider it meaningful to have mine is one of the greatest compliments I could have ever received.

Three months later, Zig Ziglar sent me this endorsement for my book:

> Jason Frenn offers a clear, easy-to-follow-and-implement plan for breaking through the barriers that might be holding you back from the freedom and success you desire. He shares his own and others' stories in a friendly, conversational style that is sure to encourage and inspire.
> —Zig Ziglar, Author and Motivational Teacher

Of all the endorsements I've received over the years, Mr. Ziglar's is one of the most important to me. Eighteen months later, I became a corporate affiliate speaker for the Ziglar Corporation.[2]

Let me ask you a question. What do you do in the face of *no*? There is a fine line between being persistent and being rude. Regardless of what you do when negotiating, moving past your barriers, overcoming objections, or dealing with a circumstance that seems impossible, never burn a bridge. You never know when circumstances will change or when people will change their minds.

One thing I've learned from Ziglar is that people will seldom admit to changing their minds in a negotiation. As he puts it, "Instead, they make a decision based on a new piece of information." Getting someone to change their mind is like getting them to admit they were wrong. Most people hate to admit it. They will, however, make a decision based upon new insights.

Another important gesture in breaking your barriers is a no-strings-attached offer. I try and find something that people like, want, or need, and if it is within my power to get it for them, I am glad to offer it. Why? When you give someone what they want, you build up credits in the account you have with them. The more credits you have in your account, the easier it is to make a withdrawal. Many times we ask a favor of someone (withdrawal) and have nothing in our account with them. They don't actually say, "Sorry, there are insufficient funds in your account," but that is exactly what they mean when they deny our request. Make sure you have sufficient funds in the account from which you want to make a withdrawal.

Let me add that if nothing else works, at least get a

commitment to revisit the issue at a future date. People change positions. They have paradigm shifts. They discover new information. Social trends have a powerful influence over people. The debate of social ethics changes the fabric of society in ways you can never imagine. Think about it. One hundred years ago women didn't have the legal right to vote. African Americans were forced to use different drinking fountains and sit in different seats than Caucasians. People confined to wheelchairs had limited access to public buildings. There were virtually no female CEOs, justices, or politicians. Fifty years ago the same could be said for most minorities. If society can change so drastically in half a century, imagine what the next fifty years will hold. And you, my friend, are just the person to help break the glass ceiling. You are a perfect candidate to pave the way for others. So be the leader. Be the persuader. Become what you are destined to be, and don't let anyone hold you back or tell you it can't be done.

Practical Steps for Breaking Your Glass Ceiling

As we bring this chapter to a close, I want to leave you with three simple yet powerful concepts to help move you to the next level and reach your highest potential. First and foremost, consult your physician, then do whatever you can to exercise on a regular basis. You don't have to join a gym. There are creative inexpensive ways to get your body in shape. Family therapists, cardiologists, medical doctors, psychiatrists, and psychologists all agree that people who exercise regularly tend to be healthier than those who don't. If you plan on becoming all that you're destined to be, you must stop treating your body like a trash can. Treat it like a billion-dollar investment. Eating less allows you to lose weight, and exercise builds stamina and tones your body. So I encourage you to do both.

Second, find a way to become wise in your approach to breaking your barriers. Read the book of Proverbs in the Bible. Spend time with or learn from those who have broken barriers similar to yours. Read the story of how Roger Bannister broke the four-minute barrier for running the mile or how we managed to put a human being on the moon. Study those who have overcome insurmountable odds to reach their greatest potential. Don't aim to be highly intelligent. Strive to be incredibly wise.

Finally, check your motives to ensure that you want to break the barriers for the right reason. If your heart is conflicted because you are hiding an ulterior motive, you won't be able to function at optimal levels morally, emotionally, physically, mentally, or professionally. If your heart is in the right place, your conscience will empower you to make the right decisions and give you the strength to implement them.

My wife and I have three daughters. I tell them there are no glass ceilings. Of course there are roads more difficult than others, but all in all, there are no impossibilities. I tell them to work harder than everyone else because that's what is best for them. I refuse to allow them to think they are victims of a biased system. Instead, I tell them to break the molds, overcome the barriers, and shatter whatever ceiling is preventing them from soaring.

I tell them that now is the greatest time in history to be alive. Anyone can conquer a giant. Anyone can overcome an obstacle. Anyone can shatter a glass ceiling. Anyone can break barriers. Simply discover your points of leverage and muster the courage to use that leverage to your advantage.

This chapter is about how to move forward when you feel

stuck. It's about discovering your greatest asset—the way you think. It's about capitalizing on your leverage, the power you have over something that other people want. Finally, this chapter aims to give you hope when all you hear is the word no. With these lessons under your belt, you can focus in chapter 6 on the five most common objections, obstacles, and rejections to every transaction.

Questions for discussion or personal reflection:

1. What is preventing you from changing your world with your product or idea? What is holding you back from leading your organization, making millions, or simply elevating your family to a whole new standard of living?

2. What is your greatest asset? What are some of the things you need to change in order to take better care of it? Why is it so important?

3. Where do you have the most leverage? How can you best use it in reaching your greatest potential?

4. How do you analyze the wants of those with whom you are negotiating? What is the process through which you discover what is sacred or highly important to them? Do you find it difficult to discover what motivates them?

5. Why is making a no-strings-attached offer important in establishing trust? What do you do when your boss, client, or customer simply says no? Why is it imperative that you do not burn any bridges?

6. What's the most important thing you've learned in this chapter?

Chapter 6

OVERCOMING OBSTACLES, OBJECTIONS, AND REJECTIONS

Successful salespeople, entrepreneurs, educators, and leaders are consistent and effective in breaking their barriers. They know the art of dealing with objections and obstacles. All the qualities of great leadership and communication that we discussed in the first two sections of this book are imperative, but they are not enough. Unless we learn to overcome the barriers we face, we will never fully develop the power to persuade and lead people to transformational decisions.

Consider the sales professional. She must convincingly overcome objections in order to sell effectively. The entrepreneur must convince investors that he has a clear plan to overcome challenges and potential setbacks. Even teachers, bank managers, advisors, and contractors must learn to overcome rejections and counterarguments. Regardless of the profession, a vast majority of us face some sort of barrier, and if we're going to reach our fullest potential we cannot hide or stick our heads in the sand. We can't afford to take a chance that everything will simply work out. We must face the thing that prevents us from moving upward and make the objection work in our favor. How? That is the focus of this chapter.

If you are learning the leadership and communication skills we discussed in the first two sections of this book, inevitably you stand at the door of incredible opportunities. You, my friend, are approaching a level of effectiveness that few people ever attain. So press forward, because what you will discover in the following pages will have a positive effect on your

OVERCOMING OBSTACLES, OBJECTIONS, AND REJECTIONS

professional and personal life. In this chapter, we will discuss the five most prominent objections and how to turn them into the reason people should follow you toward transformational decisions. The first one is no need.

1. I Have No Need

"Why in the world would I buy that?" I said. "I see absolutely no need to buy a bra for my car."

"A grille cover protects the front of your vehicle from large insects, road hazards, and small gravel kicked up from cars driving ahead of you," the salesperson said.

No matter how much he suggested it was a good idea to buy the accessory, I kept saying, "I don't see the need for it."

I was at the lot buying my first new car, a Honda CRX. I was excited about my purchase and nervous all at the same time. I was especially conscious of not allowing anyone to sell me something I didn't need (an extended warranty, fancy floor mats, pin striping, and in this case a car bra).

In the introduction to this book I stated that every attempted transaction has a seller and a buyer. The seller persuades the buyer that she should buy or the buyer persuades the seller that she shouldn't buy. When I drove off the lot of the dealership with my new car, I definitely convinced the seller that I was not buying the leather protector for the front of my car. *I've already spent more money than I wanted. There's no need to spend more,* I thought.

Two days later, I was driving down a smooth thoroughfare at nine o'clock at night with my hot new sporty vehicle. The street had three lanes in each direction and was in a nicer part of town without any traffic whatsoever. I came up over the top

120

of a slight hill driving approximately fifty miles per hour when suddenly the car dropped about eight inches. The asphalt ended and I entered a construction zone. There had been no warning signs. By the time I realized what had happened, I was driving on dirt, and it was too late. Suddenly I saw a red plastic tube standing upright about seventy-five feet ahead, and I had no way of swerving to avoid it without losing control of the vehicle. The three-foot bright red traffic pylon with reflectors riveted to the upper third nearly snapped in half when I hit it head-on. The eighteen-inch foam base and lower half of the tube wrapped underneath the bumper while the top half slammed into the hood, leaving a nice scratch and three subtle dents where the rivet heads attached to the reflector material.

When I pulled over and looked at the damage, I couldn't believe it. No merge right sign. No lighted warning. Nothing. My first thought was *I'm going to march into city hall and demand they fix my car.* However, the $250 expense for taking the city to small claims court, taking off work with a loss of wages, and the difficulty of proving that they hadn't put up a warning sign prevented me from doing so. The second thing that went through my head was *there must be some sort of a conspiracy to sell car bras.*

After a day or two, I took my vehicle to the body shop and then went back to the dealership and bought the bra. Of course, I didn't mention a thing to the sales representative. After all, I still had a smidgen of pride, albeit very little at that moment.

There is a reason people buy insurance policies. There is a reason they take precautions. And yes, there is a reason they buy grille covers for their cars. What I thought would never be a legitimate need suddenly became one. This happens all the time. Ask any wedding coordinator, mechanic, insurance agent,

Overcoming Obstacles, Objections, and Rejections

minister, doctor or lawyer. Many times people can't see a need for something until they are faced with a different reality.

If you want to be a powerful persuader you must learn to overcome objections. You do this by helping people discover a different reality. Help them see the need for something even when it isn't obvious. This is especially true if you are a sales representative, preacher, teacher, contractor, or coach. Here are a couple of ways to help people to see the need.

First, tell stories of those who didn't plan for the inevitable or didn't see the need. When someone says, "Why should I believe it?" or "Why should I buy that?" or "I see no reason for that," you can respond with a testimony of someone who experienced a loss as a result of not buying into your idea. Better yet, share an example of someone who followed your suggestion and experienced a breakthrough as a result.

Second, help them discover the necessities. Many times, people are unaware of their needs. Why is that? They cannot see the future. They cannot see the repercussions of their actions or the actions of others. They cannot discern the potential in their life or the possibilities that await them. One way to help them see these things is by asking What if . . . For example, What if you could _____ (fill in the blank), would _____ (fill in the blank with the thing or idea you're presenting) help you? Or, What would happen to your life if _____ (fill in the blank)? Help them see the possibilities of taking action or the dangers of not acting. Help them imagine the peace of mind they'll experience when they move forward with your idea, product, or solution. Help them see a need for something by painting a different reality.

2. I Have No Money

"Young man, my wife has been in and out of the hospital and hasn't worked in eighteen months. My children are heading to college in two years. Our house payments are beyond what we can afford. My business has been significantly down, and to make matters worse, our two vehicles are old and break down constantly." Jim, a middle-aged man, shook his head and then looked sternly at the insurance agent and continued, "What makes you think I can afford an expensive policy?"

The agent said, "The coverage is very comprehensive, affordable, and . . ."

"I can't afford it!" Jim interrupted before the young agent could finish his sentence.

"One hundred dollars a month for additional life insurance? Are you crazy?" The forty-three-year-old man was resolute. The agent didn't say a word. He opened his folder, pulled out the contract, and laid his pen across the middle of the top page and slid it half way across the table. He glanced up and said, "Would you like the half a million dollar policy or the $1 million policy?"

"Haven't you heard a thing I've said? Haven't you been listening?" Jim replied.

"Oh, I have sir. I've heard everything you've said, and that's what concerns me. I don't think you've heard yourself."

"What do you mean?" Jim asked.

"Your wife's on disability. You have two teenagers heading to college. Your business has been hit hard in the recession. You're up to your neck in mortgage payments, and your vehicles are in the repair shop on a regular basis. Is that correct?"

"Yes," Jim answered.

Overcoming Obstacles, Objections, and Rejections

"Considering all that you're facing, if something else happens, you and your family will lose everything. An accident, fire, or personal injury can set anyone back. However, if something happens to you, your family will never recover. No college for your children, no house for your wife, and a future plagued with bankruptcy and mounting bills. The future, as you see it, will be altered for decades. I'm trying to help you prevent that."

The agent didn't blink. He just looked at Jim with deep concern. After several long seconds, Jim finally looked down, pressed his lips together, and calmly said, "What will the monthly payments be for the $1 million policy?"

The agent saw Jim's objection as the very reason for buying the policy. If one more calamity, accident, or even death were to occur, the family would have been pushed to a level of unrecoverable financial trauma. Powerful persuaders see beyond the smokescreens to the most effective solution. They come alongside those who are stuck in life and help them break free. They help them see the remedy when answers seem impossible to find. Powerful persuaders must empathize, rationalize, and strategize if they are going to overcome the financial objections.

When faced with a financial objection, first learn to empathize with those you wish to serve. Understand their frustrations, pain, or discontent. Or capture their hope, aspirations, and dreams. Grasping the feeling of not being where they want to be helps you lead others to transformational decisions. It helps you understand the emotional struggles they face. Understanding their hopes or frustrations equips you to be a problem solver.

It's important, however, that you don't simply empathize. That's where many professionals make a crucial error. If you let your customer's frustration overwhelm you, then you too will become blind to the possible solutions. So be rational. Think clearly as you come alongside them in the midst of their challenges, frustrations, or unfulfilled dreams. People need to feel that you have solid answers and that you see a solution well enough to help them when they are uncertain about their future.

Finally, learn to strategize. Learn to problem solve and navigate through the turbulence so that you can provide the best solution for everyone. Don't provide a solution if you are not completely confident in it. If you see that your solution doesn't work nearly as well as your competitor's, then suggest that they investigate other options. People remember when we place their needs before our own. When you demonstrate an honest strategy, you build employment security for your future.

Of all the obstacles and objections that exist, *I have no money* is by far the most common. However, I have discovered that people find the time to do what they want to do. They manage to find a way to go where they want to go. With few exceptions, people find the money to buy what they truly want to buy. The question is *how desperately do they want it?* Help people to want it, and they will find the money to buy it. Henry Ford did that with a car. General Electric did that with the refrigerator. Apple did that with the iPhone. From the onset, these items were not cheap, but people acquired the money to purchase them. Today, people continue to buy what seems beyond their means. Why? Because they want it.

3. I'm Not in a Hurry

When people have an urgent need, persuasion is easy. When they don't, leading them to transformational decisions becomes more difficult. Such was the case when my wife and I purchased our first home. We had lived overseas for a number of years, and then returned to Southern California in December 2004 to visit family for the holidays. Cindee and I were driving home after seeing a movie when we spotted a real estate sign with a familiar name on it. Bob and Sandy Birtwell were lifelong friends and Bob had been my regional manager when I sold paper at Moore Business Forms sixteen years earlier. I immediately called the number listed on the sign, and Bob answered the phone.

I said, "Bob, I am sorry to call you so late. To be honest, I thought your voice mail would pick up." He said, "Actually, Sandy and I are in Miami. We just went to the national championship college football game at the Orange Bowl. We're just getting back from the stadium."

I said, "Please call me when you return to Southern California. Even though we are not in the market to buy a home today, when we return to live in the United States in six months, we'd like to see if we can afford a home." He said, "We'll be back in two days."

When they returned Sandy arranged to show us some properties and educate us on how to buy a house. We looked at about ten different properties. Some were wonderful but too expensive. Others were well priced but not suitable for us. The last property we scheduled to view was out of our price range.

As soon as we pulled up to the house, I knew I was in trouble. It was beautiful. The entry was gorgeous. The living room had vaulted ceilings and the lighting was picturesque. My wife and Sandy walked to the top of the stairs while I followed several steps behind. When they reached the second floor, Sandy turned around, looked at Cindee, and said, "Can you say *loft*?"

Cindee's eyes lit up. They both understood the significance of additional footage. Two hundred extra square feet would add tens of thousands of dollars to the value of the home. The cost to put in a loft is minimal compared to the benefit and monetary value it would yield.

The only thing that I could think was, *We're not in a hurry, and we don't need a home now. We're on a fact-finding mission.* After looking at the different rooms, admiring the layout, and figuring out which room would belong to which child, we headed out to the car.

Sandy asked, "What do you think?"

I said, "It's beautiful. It's everything we want and need in a home."

She said, "Well, I believe we can offer twenty thousand dollars less than what the owner is asking."

"Uh, I think we should hold on a minute," I responded. "We won't be back in the United States for another six months. We can't buy a home and leave it unoccupied for such a long period of time."

"Jason, I wouldn't suggest anything to you that wouldn't be in your best interest. If you feel this home is a great fit for your family, perhaps we should ask how we can make it work for you."

"I don't know, Sandy." I was doubtful. "How can we make mortgage payments while we still live overseas? We can't make two payments."

"You can ask the owner to give you a longer escrow. That way, the house won't be vacant that long nor will you be responsible for as many monthly payments. The owner might even sell you the house and rent a couple of months from you in order to find a place of her own. Jason, this house is one block

127

OVERCOMING OBSTACLES, OBJECTIONS, AND REJECTIONS

from the high school where your daughters can attend. It's a turnkey. If you put in a loft, the value will rise considerably. This is a great opportunity that will not be here when you move back in six months."

Cindee and I talked it over, and after five minutes we said to her, "We'll tell you what. Offer twenty thousand dollars less than the asking price, and make the offer contingent on a sixty-day escrow. If the owner needs more time, we'll be open to renting the property back to her for up to another month."

I never thought for one moment the owner would take our offer. I was convinced she would reject it.

That afternoon, Sandy called me. "You won't believe what happened. The other realtor met with the owner, and she accepted all of your conditions. She made no counter offer. She had no stipulations. She will consider renting back from you after you open escrow with a deposit." I nearly dropped the phone. Six months later we flew into LAX and drove directly to our first home.

I often wonder how we bought our home, especially when we were not in a hurry. We were simply in the process of educating ourselves. Sandy knew what we wanted, what we needed, and helped us see a window of opportunity. She knew that with a sense of urgency we would be much more likely to move forward with the purchase. I am glad she did. The home proved to be in an ideal location for our young family.

All of our girls walked to the elementary school and high school. Our home was located within a mile of a major regional shopping mall and a hospital. We had everything a family could need within five minutes of our home.

Like Sandy, people who demonstrate a power to persuade help others see a window of opportunity. They help them feel a sense of urgency. Whether it's a limited offer or limited supply, those who are highly effective at overcoming objections draw attention to a possible loss. Remember this important rule when it comes to persuasion. The fear of loss is greater than the desire for gain. People hate missing out on something wonderful. Even worse, they hate losing or feeling humiliated.

When you are faced with the objection of *no hurry,* find a way to help people see their wonderful window of opportunity. Create a sense of urgency. You might even point out an incentive if they act soon. For example, you might say, "If you act now, you can avoid additional costs." Or, "If you agree to move forward today, you'll get the second one at a discount." Or even, "Don't miss out on this great opportunity for _____ (fill in the blank)." Of course, you need to contextualize these phrases for your field or occupation. Nonetheless, the idea is the same. You want to help those you serve to sense the urgency of acting sooner rather than later. If you truly believe that you offer the best solution, help others see the wonderful opportunity that is before them.

4. I Have No Desire

Arturo left his Costa Rican family and headed north to Mexico. His goal was to reach the United States and live the American dream. After making arrangements, the seventeen-year-old landed at the Mexico City airport and took a bus to the Tijuana-California border. He had no visa, no passport, and hardly any money. After two days of living on the streets of Tijuana, he found someone who for a small fee would "escort" him across the border.

The next evening the escort led a group of aspiring young

Overcoming Obstacles, Objections, and Rejections

people through a small hole in the large wall that separated the two countries. As soon as everyone was through, they paid the man, who quickly retreated through the hole to Mexican soil. The others briskly walked toward the slight glow coming from the city of San Diego when suddenly blinding floodlights attached to the top of four-wheel-drive vehicles relentlessly followed their every movement. "This is the United States Border Patrol," they heard. "Stay where you are. You are under arrest."

Arturo experienced a fear much greater than anything he'd ever felt in his young life. Sitting in the back of the Border Patrol vehicle, he felt hopeless and ashamed. "What will my parents think?" he wondered. Because of his age, instead of the San Diego County Jail, the authorities took him to a youth detention center. They registered his belongs, and opened his cell door. When he walked in, he felt there was some sort of mistake.

His cell had carpet, air conditioning, cable TV, and a private bathroom. His room had a small window through which he had a view of the San Diego airport. The next day during mealtimes, he discovered he could go back for seconds. A doctor came once a week, and a chaplain offered church services as well. One day, his uncle David came and offered to pay his bail. Arturo responded, "No thanks!"

"Why not?"

"I live better here than I do in my home country."

It took Arturo's uncle two days to convince him that there was more freedom outside of prison than inside. Even then, Arturo still was skeptical. Up until the first night he spent outside of jail, he had no desire to taste freedom. He was content and truly thought he was living the American dream. Unfortunately,

Power To Persuade

many people feel content right where they are and are clueless that they are missing out on so much.

So what do you do if you're dealing with someone who has no desire to follow you, buy from you, receive your counsel, or accept the idea you're presenting? Of all the objections, obstacles, and rejections, *no desire* is one of the most difficult to manage.

In Arturo's case, his uncle had to find out what his nephew wanted. He wanted to live the American dream. That dream is not about living behind bars even if all your basic needs are covered. Instead, it's based upon three things: religious freedom, political freedom, and financial freedom. As long as Arturo was in jail, he didn't have any freedom. The only way he could experience the dream he always wanted to live was to see that his situation was unacceptable.

This is precisely what powerful persuaders help others to do. They discover what people need and help them see that the status quo is unacceptable. They help people bridge the gap between where they are and where they need to be in order to experience the desires of their heart.

Inevitably when the pain of staying the same is greater than the pain caused by the proposed change, people move toward a better solution. Persuasive solutions only work when people can see a pathway to reach them, a pathway that brings them closer to their dreams and the solutions that meet their needs.

If you're going to overcome the objections, obstacles, and barriers that prevent you from leading people to transformational decisions, you must show people a better way even when they are content to stay where they are. If you're into fitness, show people who don't work out a picture of a healthy heart and contrast it with an unhealthy heart. The same is true with finances, family, and education. Show people a better life with what you're presenting, and the concept of *not needing it* will begin to dissipate quickly.

In addition to finding out what people's needs and desires are, find out if their lack of interest is based upon the fact that they don't know what's available. Many times people are not interested in buying a black grille cover for their car because they don't see the need for it, but they might buy a white one because it looks good as an accessory.

Many times people don't make a choice because they don't know what's available. For example, some adults would earn their master's degree if they knew that night and weekend classes were available. People would buy their dream home if they could discover unconventional financing. Some people would quit their nine to five job if they knew how to start their own business. People need to see the options and possibilities that are available. Once you help to open their eyes, they are able to see the tremendous opportunities open to them.

5. I Don't Trust You

For as long as I can remember, I wanted to buy a Mustang GT. Several years ago I started a savings account and whenever possible made small contributions. Finally, I had enough funds set aside, and I was anxious to buy a model that was one or two years old.

I will never forget walking onto a dealership lot and looking over the four models that had less than thirteen thousand miles on the odometer. After about ten minutes, I realized something strange. No sales representatives approached me. When I looked toward the showroom, three middle-aged men were sitting outside the doors conversing about something humorous. I walked over and patiently waited for them to acknowledge me. I said, "Excuse me. Do you gentlemen work here?"

"We sure do," one of them barked out. "How can we help you?"

"Well, I'm interested in a used Mustang," I said.

Without hesitating, the potbellied sarcastic fellow leaned back in his chair and said, "You're up champ," as he nodded to the youngest one in the group.

The younger man said nothing. He just pointed at his own chest and mouthed, "Me?" The big one nodded affirmatively.

The man slowly got up and extended his hand. "My name is Josh," and to protect his identity, I have changed his name. With enthusiasm he said, "You are going to be my first customer."

I said, "Your first customer today?"

"I wish!" he replied. "No, my first customer ever."

"You mean since you started working here, right?" I asked.

"Oh, yeah. Of course."

Thinking that he was in his first week as a car salesman I asked, "How long have you been working?"

"Six months," he said nonchalantly.

Six months I thought. *You obviously have skinny children.* What salesman stays on the job for six months without a sale? What company keeps a salesman who hasn't sold anything in half a year? What manager doesn't train his or her sales force? Zig Ziglar makes a great statement in his teachings: "There's only one thing worse than training people and then losing them, and that is not training them and keeping them."[2]

I knew one thing. If I had any doubt whatsoever about buying the car, this salesman wouldn't have the wherewithal to overcome my objections.

Overcoming Obstacles, Objections, and Rejections

"Which Mustang are you interested in?" Josh asked.

"The red one," I replied.

"The red one? Why that one?" he asked. "It will only attract highway patrolmen. Don't you know that red is the worst color car to own on the road? Besides, you should get a new one. They last longer."

For a moment, I thought I was going crazy. Right before my eyes, Josh was perfecting the art of losing the sale. I've seen many people do stupid things to turn off a buyer who was ready to make the purchase, but none compared to him.

I said, "Listen, I am interested in this vehicle because it has low mileage, it's a California Special, and it's the right year. Besides, the reviews are very positive." He forced his lips to the furthest left he could then rubbed his chin. Then he said, "Tell you what. Let me make a call to my manager and see what I can do for you." I am not really sure why he would want to call his manager, and if the potbellied fellow was the manager, I definitely didn't want the two of them talking over a potential deal with me.

As he made the call he said, "Hey, it's me." Then he lowered his voice. "He's interested in the red one. Yeah, I know it's used," he softly said. "I know I won't make the same commission. Okay, I'll tell him." He closed his flip phone and looked at me and said, "Are you sure you don't want this brand new black one over here?"

As to not be rude, I said to him, "Tell you what. I'll think about it." I had no intention of returning. Was the red car a good match for me? Absolutely. Was the price right? Yes. Was it the right time in my life? I believe so. So why didn't I buy the car? I lost all trust in the representative. After ten minutes, I completely understood why he hadn't sold a car in six months.

I still want to own a four-hundred-plus horsepower driving machine. When it comes to vehicles, though, trust is one of the most important aspects of the deal.

Most people buy from those they trust. A woman generally marries a man she feels she can trust. A child makes his first leap into a swimming pool because he trusts his father will catch him. We fly with airlines we trust. We listen to the minister we trust. We submit to the doctor we trust. We learn from the professors we trust. Think about it for a moment. Is there anyone you buy or learn from that you don't trust? Do you follow anyone you don't trust?

How can you establish trust with those you are trying to persuade? Is it possible to do so without being manipulative? I believe you can, especially if you remember the following three important principles. They will help you establish trust with others quickly and effectively.

First, be transparent about your family. If you sincerely love your spouse and children, that is a huge asset. People are much more likely to trust a man, for example, who cares about his wife and children. Why is that? It shows that he is not entirely self-centered. Think about it. The term *family man* sounds positive and trustworthy. It gives a person great credibility. The same is true for a woman, grandparent, or even a teenager. When your family members support you, it is a positive reference for you.

For that reason, whenever possible I take my wife and daughters with me and introduce them when I am making a presentation for the first time. The ladies in my life give me more credibility than any words that come out of my mouth or polished presentation I can make. For some reason, strangers are likely to extend trust when the family seems united behind your cause.

Second, use testimonials that highlight your service, product, or idea. Mention the individuals who have experienced a breakthrough, especially if they are known by those you're trying to reach. Any endorsement can help open doors with people who struggle with trust. I've obtained some wonderful endorsements over the years, and I guard them in a vault. I put them on my website. I share them in newsletters. I print them on the back covers of my books. At first, people may or may not believe your words, but they are much more likely to believe the endorsement coming from familiar people or companies.

Third, don't ask for anything. Instead, ask to serve. I've quoted Zig Ziglar several times and it merits repeating one of his statements here. "You can have everything in life you want if you will just help enough other people get what they want."[1] Jesus summed it up this way, "If anyone wants to be first, he must be the very last, and the servant of all" (Mark 9:35). Look for a way to help people without any strings attached. Offer them a service, a gift, or something they need and ask nothing in return. At first, people will wonder. Your attitude should simply be, "I am here to help as many people as I can." The more people you help, the greater the return on investment. It's the law of reciprocity. You will reap whatever you sow. So sow generously into the lives of your clients, customers, followers, and those you aim to serve.

The greatest persuaders in life don't see objections, they see opportunities. When they hear the word no, they don't interpret that as a *no* rejection but rather a *know* as in "I need to *know* more about what you are presenting before I make a decision." They do not take rejection personally. They see it as a chasm or distance between two ideas that with time, information, and reason, will join together to create transformational decisions.

Practical Steps to Overcome Objections, Obstacles, and Rejections

When you are faced with an objection, focus on the most central desire and need of those with whom you're dealing. Is the obstacle based upon the lack of need, money, urgency, desire, or trust? Odds are it's one of these five reasons. Once you narrow it down, verbalize it to the person(s) to whom you are presenting your idea or product. Then ask them, "If there were a way to save you money (in the case of a financial objection), would you be willing to consider moving forward with this option? Or is there something else?" If it's another type of objection, then mention that one in a similar sentence. For example, "If I could show you how moving forward with this idea or product would fulfill an important need you have (in the case of a no apparent need), would that be something you'd be interested in?" These types of questions simply narrow down the objections to help you see where the true resistance is coming from. Anytime people have the opportunity to talk about how they feel, you will gain incredible insights on how to better lead them to transformational decisions.

The number one objection to nearly any sale is lack of money. People use the phrase *I can't afford it* more than any other reason for not making a purchase. The most difficult objection to overcome is "I don't need it." Why do people buy something they don't need? Odds are they won't, unless of course they want it. Want is a much more powerful motivator than *need*. So if they don't need what you're presenting, look for a way to help them *want* it.

The third most difficult objection is a lack of urgency. When people have time to make a decision, that can be a good thing

OVERCOMING OBSTACLES, OBJECTIONS, AND REJECTIONS

for them, but at the same time, it could be a curse. How could it be a curse? When people don't feel urgency, they don't feel the pressure to take advantage of a great opportunity when it comes their way. They walk by one open door after another without committing to any of them. As a powerful persuader, you must help the people you serve see that once-in-a-lifetime open door so that they don't miss out on a life-changing decision.

Many times people don't move forward with a decision simply because they don't fully trust the one presenting the product, service, or idea. It's not that they don't have the funds or the desire. They simply don't feel comfortable entering into a buyer-seller, teacher-student, leader-follower relationship. Once trust is established, you become an ally instead of an adversary. You become an asset instead of a liability. You become a valuable resource.

As we bring this chapter to a close, remember to clarify each objection or obstacle to the person you are dealing with. Ask him or her if their reason for not moving forward (price, timing, style, appeal, trust, or whatever the reason may be) is their only hesitation. If so, you can simply ask that if you find a reasonable solution to their concern would they be willing to move forward with a positive decision. Deal with each objection or obstacle in this manner. Then, you can move forward to the next stage in powerful persuasion, *the close*.

Questions for discussion or personal reflection:

1. What are some of the ways you can overcome a lack of need? How can you help people see a potential need that they had no idea existed?

2. What are some of the ways you have helped others overcome their financial barriers when making a decision? In your opinion, why do people become entrenched when facing a financial objection? What can you do to help them?

3. Why is time important when leading people to transformational decisions? What can you do to make a lack of urgency and desire work in your favor?

4. What have you done in the past to gain the trust of those you aim to serve?

5. What's the most important thing you've learned in this chapter?

Section IV

Persuasive Closing

Chapter 7

BECOME A POWERFUL CLOSER

Jeremy slid the piece of paper across the table. The bottom of the contract read *$3 million*. He felt there was a fifty-fifty chance that Mr. Zimmerman would agree to the deal. It was the longest three seconds of the entire sales process.

Mr. Zimmerman looked at Jeremy and said, "I have no idea how you're getting me to sign, but for some reason, I am. You sold me. " He then pulled out a pen from his inside coat pocket and signed the contract.

Jeremy wanted to jump five feet in the air but somehow contained his elation. Instead, he proudly grinned and said, "Mr. Zimmerman, congratulations, you are the proud owner of a jet."

After Mr. Zimmerman took possession of the aircraft, Jeremy decided to revisit the sales process with the multimillionaire. Taking a significant risk, he called him to ask a simple question. "Mr. Zimmerman," he said, "I know you said that you had no idea why you decided to buy from me, but I know you are much more astute than that. I want you to help me become the very best sales representative I can. Please be honest. Why did you grant me your business?"

Mr. Zimmerman paused for a moment and said, "You know, I guess you tied everything together well, and because of that, I trusted you. I felt that you would do what you said you were going to do."

Building trust with those we aim to serve is imperative. Without trust, we have no hope of leading them to transformational decisions. Without leading them to the point of making a decision, we have no hope of cementing or closing our transaction. Without mastering the art of closing, we have no hope of gaining their business or completing the purpose we set out to accomplish with them.

This final section is essential to the art of persuasion. It aims to help you become a powerful closer. This chapter deals with the four areas that powerful closers master when leading people toward the best solution. The first area is having a clear idea of where the customer is in the persuasion process.

1. The Right Summary

A close friend invited me to hear a great communicator during one of the regional conventions for his organization. I will never forget the dynamic and challenging keynote address that evening. Richard, the CEO and president of a multinational organization had me on the edge of my seat. I was so impressed that the following Monday I wrote a letter and told him how inspiring his presentation was. I mentioned that although I had spoken all over the world, there were few people who kept me engaged like he did. I shared a link on my YouTube channel of a bilingual event we held at a major convention center in Southern California. I finished the letter with the following statement: "I believe the best years for your organization and its wonderful consultants are fast approaching, and I would like to share with you how I might be of assistance. All I need is a few minutes of your time at a location that works for you. My office is close to your corporate offices. My cell number is listed below. Please feel free to call."

Within an hour of the letter's arrival at his corporate office,

Richard called me. "Tell me, Jason, in what way do you feel you can help us reach the next level in sales?" he asked.

I said, "I believe I can help your organization increase the amount of sales your consultants are making by helping them become better closers."

"How do you intend to do that?" he asked.

"I would like to share my insights at your next convention, that is, as your keynote speaker." Considering that Richard didn't know me nor had he heard of me prior to the arrival of my letter, I am surprised he didn't laugh at my boldness. Still, he was a straightforward leader, and I knew he would appreciate someone who cut to the chase.

He responded, "Later, we can discuss your credentials, but let me ask you right up front. What is your fee for a keynote address?" Notice that he didn't ask me what I would have been willing to receive in exchange for my services. Instead, he simply asked what the price was.

"How many consultants do you expect at your national convention?" I asked. "Ten thousand," he replied. Without hesitating I said, "Twenty thousand dollars."

"Jason, I like you," he said, "and I am glad you didn't say $1,500. If you had, I would know that you didn't have the experience we're looking for. Before I called, I watched your bilingual presentation at the Anaheim Convention Center. I enjoyed it. However, I need more assurance that what you will share will be worth your speaking fee as well as highly beneficial for our consultants." I knew at that moment the task to persuade him was growing more difficult, but it was still possible.

I paused for a moment and said, "You mentioned during your speech last Friday that you felt that you offered a superior product. You also alluded to the fact that your percentage of new business sales is decreasing. Is that the case?"

"Yes it is," he replied.

"In most cases, that is because representatives struggle with the way they are closing. More than half of sales calls end without an attempt to close the sale. Further, the national closing rate is about twenty-five percent."

"That is what our VP of sales tells me," he muttered.

I continued, "You've indicated that you want to blow away your competition, and for that reason you want new sales to increase substantially. Would you say that is true?"

"I would agree," he said.

"I have an idea that I think will solve your problem and eliminate any doubt of how beneficial my keynote presentation would be to your consultants. To find out, it won't cost you a dime. Would you be open to that?"

"Yes, I would," he said.

"Why don't I join you on your next training call? I will share three principles of a series I call 'Killer Closes'. When the call is finished and consultants begin to put into practice what they've learned, you'll receive feedback and you can monitor the results of their efforts. At that point, you can make a decision regarding my participation in your next convention. If you want to extend to me the invitation to speak, and you are not fully satisfied with my presentation, I will refund my fee minus my expenses. Does that sound fair to you, Richard?"

"Absolutely," he answered enthusiastically.

Three weeks later, I was on a nationwide sales training conference call with thousands of representatives who listened to the same principles I will be sharing in the next chapter of this book. The conference call opened the door for me to speak and train representatives across the nation. Through it all, I learned a valuable lesson. Being straightforward and giving people a summary of where they are and where they want to go helps them clearly see the decision that will bring transformation to their lives and businesses.

Over the years, I discovered that effective closers give us a simple and straightforward summation of how we got to where we are. They set up the close with precision and clarity. Regardless of their profession—a highly skilled loan officer, sales representative, motivational speaker, entrepreneur, or trial lawyer—they make a succinct statement that clearly spells out where we are in the process as we ponder our decision.

They do this in a simple sentence or something more comprehensive, depending upon their field. For the purposes of brevity, I will share what are simple summary statements. A powerful summary touches on our frustration, challenge, problem, or aspiration, and it reminds us of our desire for acquisition, improvement, advancement, victory, or healing. An example of a powerful summary statement is "You've mentioned that you want to move ahead because you feel stuck." Or, "I can see how you would feel frustrated with your car constantly breaking down, and you want to be free from the worry of being stranded on the road." Another summary statement is "You seem concerned about your financial future, and you want the peace of mind that no matter what may come your way you'll always have enough capital to maintain the lifestyle you want."

If you are making a presentation to a major corporation to help them increase their revenue, you might say, "You've indicated that you want to blow away your competition, and for that reason you want new sales to increase substantially."

These statements aim to lead those we serve to say yes. If your customer, prospect, or client looks puzzled after such a statement, you have not diagnosed the situation correctly. In this case, you need to verify what their needs and desires are. If they say yes, you're ready to move on to the next crucial stage in powerful closing. The right summary sets up the *right question*.

2. The Right Question

Ron recently had taken over as the new CEO of the organization. For nearly three decades his company was one of the most profitable in the industry. With time, though, they lost business to newer, more innovative companies. Their marketing department simply regurgitated old ideas, and they never embraced the technological changes of the past ten years. Ron knew that he had an eighteen-month window of opportunity to turn things around. If not, the competition would crush them, and the company would be liquidated.

Ron looked at Peter over the top of his cherrywood desk and asked, "How can I promote change throughout the organization? There are many holy grails, and people are very territorial. Besides, most of us hate change."

Ron and Peter had been friends for years. Of all the leaders Peter knew, Ron was one of the most capable. He had a plan, but he had no idea how to sell it to the most influential people in the organization.

"Tell me in general terms what the problem is," Peter said.

"Over the past thirty years, we've had a great run, but the current system is broken. Much like a car when it has high mileage, it breaks down and must be fixed," he said.

"That's a great analogy," Peter replied. "After you show them that the car is broken, you need to ask those you lead the *right question*."

"What is that?" he asked.

"Ask them if they want to break down in the middle of nowhere and then be forced to sell the car for parts to the highest bidder. Because, Ron, that is exactly what happens to companies that do not adapt to changing times. The one thing every organization has in common if they don't adapt is doom."

Ron sat back in his chair and rubbed his chin. He said, "Please continue."

"If you accurately describe the pending doom, and they see it," Peter said, "ask them if they want to alter their course. If they do, present your answer for the difficult transition your company faces."

A week later, Ron called a meeting with the directors of marketing, manufacturing, sales, and accounting. This time, he arranged the meeting room differently. Instead of having them sit in rows, he placed forty chairs in a large circle so that fewer people would be tempted to look at e-mails or social media. He started the meeting by holding up a model of a 1964 Mustang.

"This is my favorite car," he said. "It's been one of the most successful and best-selling muscle cars in the world. It has lasted well over five decades. In many ways, our company is like this vehicle. The only difference is we haven't evolved over the years like it has." Ron continued, "We haven't changed or introduced anything new in our design, products, or services."

The group sat in silence.

"Now imagine that you have never changed the oil. You've never changed the tires. You've never changed the shock absorbers. It's never had a tune up. And now, your Mustang has half a million miles on it. How long do you anticipate your car will last?"

One member of the group laughed and said, "Long enough to reach the junk yard."

"Exactly," Ron said. "It's not that we didn't buy a great car. It is one of the best. But if we don't make some significant adjustments, other car enthusiasts will break it down and use the parts for their Mustangs that they've kept in great shape over the years. Does that sound fair?"

Several group members nodded their heads.

"Do you want to watch our company disintegrate? Or do you want to do what is necessary to become the best in our industry once again?"

That was the question that changed the direction of the company. Every person in the room had a vested interested in the future of the organization. Once they understood where they were headed and understood the challenge to change, they unanimously decided to embrace Ron's plan to restructure and reinvent the company.

Asking the right question may sound simple and rudimentary, but it is essential in the process of effective closing. In order to be a powerful closer, you must tie the right question to the right summary. If you have ascertained the scenario correctly, the people you aim to serve will affirm that your summary is accurate and true. Remember, change only comes when the status quo becomes unacceptable. When the pain of staying the same is greater than the pain of change, then people will change. So if your summary statement is accurate, your question is even more important. The essence of a powerful question is simply this, "Are you interested in change?" Of course, we don't say that in every situation, but the answer to that question is what we want to know. This is why we use questions that evoke a positive answer.

Here are some examples of effective questions that awaken your customer, follower, or client to the possibilities of a transformational change:
- Are you frustrated?
- Are you satisfied with where you are in life?
- Do you want to save money?
- Are you tired of being tired?
- Do you feel this is fair?
- Do you want to make more money?
- Do you want to move up?
- Do you want to be healthy?
- Do you want peace of mind?
- Do you want to feel attractive?
- Do you want to be free?
- Do you want eternal life?

These questions are general, and you need to contextualize them for your specific circumstance or field of expertise. Once you see the needs and recognize the desires of those you serve, it's imperative that you listen to their answers. Don't simply assume that the answer to these questions is yes or that you're asking the right question.

As you present your product, idea, or solution, the following questions can help you connect it with the desires and needs of those you serve:
- Can you see how this will make you money?
- Can you see how this option will save you time?
- Do you see how this course will help move you in the direction of your dreams?
- Can you see how this home has all the qualities you're

looking for?

• Will this vehicle help you save on gas and maintenance costs?

Again, if the answer to these questions is yes you can move forward and provide the direction that your customers, followers, or clients need. The right question leads to the *right solution*.

3. The Right Solution

Zig Ziglar tells a story about a friend of his, Jay Martin, who was president of National Safety Associates (NSA). Initially, NSA sold smoke detectors for homes, but in the late 1970s they began distributing water filters, which I sold during the summer I graduated from college. One night, Jay went on a sales call with one of his young representatives who made a compelling presentation.

When the representative finished and asked the homeowner if he was interested in the smoke detection equipment, the owner sat back, crossed his arms, and said, "Son, I know you've heard about my wreck." Actually, the young salesman hadn't heard about the accident, so the older gentleman began to enlighten him.

He said, "My wife and I were driving down the road a few months ago, and a driver was passing another vehicle on the wrong side of the highway and hit us head-on. We both landed in the hospital. I was there for ten days and ever since I was released, I haven't been able to work as much. My legs are still recovering and that has affected our income. My wife was in the hospital for six weeks and by the time she was released her employer phased out her job. So our income has taken a serious hit."

The representative sat there patiently and listened to everything the homeowner conveyed. The homeowner continued, "The hospital bill was over twenty thousand dollars for both of us. I am sure the insurance will cover most of it, but they sure are putting pressure on us."

"Just a week ago, my son came back from the Navy, and the first night home he took our car and rounded a curve too fast. He lost control, went over an embankment, rammed into a service station, and smashed into an oil company sign that cost seven thousand dollars. Now I'm fairly sure that the insurance will cover my car, but I don't know if they'll cover the sign."

"Finally," he said, "if that weren't enough, last night we checked my mother-in-law into the most expensive nursing home in the county. I am sure that I'm going to wind up paying her monthly bills as well."

Most people in sales would have folded their tents and said, "Sir, my heart really goes out to you. As a matter of fact, if I had any money, I'd gladly help you out."

However, instead of feeling overwhelmed by the man's plight, the NSA representative backed away from the problem to find the best solution he could. He asked the homeowner, "In addition to those reasons sir, would there be any other reasons why you could not go ahead and install this equipment in your home to protect your family?"

The homeowner couldn't believe his ears. *Are you kidding me?* he thought. Then he slapped his leg and mockingly laughed, "No, son, those are the only reasons we cannot go ahead and purchase the equipment."

The young salesman calmly reached into his briefcase and pulled out a smoke detector and walked over to the wall. He positioned it in the ideal location, showing the homeowner how it would look on the wall. Then he said, "Sir, as best as I can tell, you now owe nearly thirty thousand dollars. Then he paused for a moment and said, "And three hundred dollars more won't make much difference at all." Then he looked the man squarely in the eye and made the statement that closed the deal. In doing so, he provided the best solution for the man and his family. "Sir," he said, "fire, under any circumstance is devastating. But in your case, it would wipe you out."

The homeowner bought the detector. Why? The representative helped him see that he couldn't endure one more tragedy. Zig Ziglar sums up the story perfectly when he tells it in his series *Secrets of Closing the Sale:* "The representative took the reasons the homeowner used to say no and turned them into the reasons why he absolutely must buy."[1]

Powerful closers understand that the right solution is hard to resist. If you present the right solution after asking the right question and assessing the circumstance accurately, it will be difficult for people to reject your idea, product, or solution.

Whether you are a lawyer, sales representative, preacher, entrepreneur, teacher, or administrator, if you are in a profession that requires persuasion, you must convey a strong conviction. Notice that I didn't say *passion*. Passion comes and goes depending upon our emotional state. A conviction is a profound sense based upon a belief. Convictions lead us to action and to verbalize our thoughts. When we open our mouths to speak, something happens in our minds that reaffirms and strengthens our beliefs. That is why couples during a wedding ceremony confess their commitment to each other before witnesses. That is why we must verbally take an oath before testifying in a court of law.

Let me ask you a couple of questions about this important

step. What *do* you believe about what you sell or present? Is there something you hold to be overwhelmingly true that you would be willing to look people in the eye and say, "I believe this is the best solution for you." Could you share your beliefs in front of your schoolmates, coworkers, or family members who don't believe as you do? It's your conviction that demonstrates that you have the best solution for the people you aim to help.

The following statements demonstrate your conviction for offering the right solution:

- This is why I suggest that you consider this as an option.
- I highly recommend that you accept this offer.
- I believe that this is the right course of action.
- This smoke detector could save your life and those of the people you love.
- Of all the possible solutions in the world, this is the best one for you.

Whether or not you choose to use these phrases or terminology, the conviction behind them is what you want to convey. You must believe in what you present. You must believe in the solution you represent. You must believe that no other option compares to yours.

If you are not one hundred percent sincere and convinced when you make that statement, you shouldn't recommend it to those you're trying to serve. If there is a hint of disingenuousness, your customer, client, or followers will sense it, and you will lose their trust.

If you accurately assess the challenge, ask the right question, and present the right solution with conviction, you can move on to the final stage in powerful closing. The right solution leads to the right call to action.

4. The Right Call to Action

John and Dennis were friends who lived in Southern California. Both of them felt the pressure of living in an expensive metropolitan area. John decided to attend a seminar on financial growth. The presenter was persuasive, and the content was compelling. He painted an accurate picture of the challenges people face with school loans, mortgages, long-term medical care for seniors, and retirement. He asked the obligating questions to which most of the audience nodded in agreement. He offered a doable plan emphasizing multiple streams of income. Then he said, "If you're interested in attaining financial freedom, feel free to visit our website and sign up for the program. I hope you do. I believe we can help you."

John wrote down the web address and took the information home to show his wife. When he walked through the front door, she said, "How was the seminar?"

"It was good. I learned a lot," he responded.

"Oh really, like what?" she asked.

"We need to increase our savings and retirement, because if we don't it could be devastating for us."

She replied, "Oh, that's sobering. Did you learn anything to avoid it?"

"We need different forms of income," he replied.

"How are we supposed to do that?" she asked.

"Good question. They want me to sign up for some service."

In a frustrated tone, she said, "Sweetheart, you said the seminar was *good*, but ever since you starting explaining it to me, it sounds depressing."

Somewhat defensive, John said, "Listen, here's the website.

If you want to learn more about their system, go check it out yourself."

"No thanks," she said. "It's probably some sort of gimmick."

About a month later, Dennis went to a financial seminar sponsored by a different investment company. The presenter covered many of the same issues people face when they grow older. He discussed college tuitions, healthcare expenses, and retirement demands. After asking the right questions and offering the right solutions, he paused and made the most important statement of the presentation. "I don't usually put people on the spot," he said, "but I believe so much in this solution for your financial future that I am going to ask you to do something out of the ordinary. If you want the keys to your financial freedom, I want you to stand to your feet right now."

About ten people quickly got up out of their chairs. Others took a few seconds. After about fifteen seconds, about half the room was standing.

"Now I want you to head over to one of the tables located on either side of this conference room and fill out the card that you see highlighted on the screen above my head. That's it. Go ahead and walk over right now even while I continue to talk."

The attendees slowly made their way to the tables, and for those who simply stood there, an assistant walked up to them and motioned in the direction of their nearest table.

The presenter continued, "Our assistants will hand you a folder with some great information regarding what you can do to avoid financial ruin. It's yours to keep even if you choose to drop out of our program. Now, before you pay a dime for this program, we want you to bring your spouse or significant other back so that the two of you can be on the same page. If you are single, you can begin the program as soon as you want."

Become A Powerful Closer

A man halfway back raised his hand, "Do I have to bring my wife back?"

"No," the presenter responded. "We simply recommend it in order to promote unity in your family."

"My wife trusts me wholeheartedly," the man replied.

"I wish mine did," another man uttered from the back. People laughed.

Dennis filled out the card, took the folder back to his wife, and brought her to the follow-up meeting. From that time forward, they have diligently worked together to secure their financial future. That was ten years ago.

Sadly, John and his wife are now divorced. In contrast, Dennis and his wife have no debt, a decent retirement account, and rental properties.

Now, I am not going to blame the presenter of the first seminar for the demise of John's marriage because he didn't have a clear call to action. I can assure you they had problems brewing for years prior to the financial seminar. However, imagine if someone came along and helped them chart out a financial course for their future. Their story might be different. After all, differences over money are the number one reason people divorce.[2]

That's why I believe a call to action must be clear. It must be heartfelt. It must be sincere. It must not be apologetic. It can't be manipulative, but it must be compassionate. Winston Churchill, Nelson Mandela, Billy Graham, Franklin D. Roosevelt, Mahatma Gandhi, Moses, and Jesus all had one powerful thing in common. They were great closers who gave people a clear call to action.

Let's reflect on John's case for a moment. Once John left the venue, convincing his wife of the merits of the program was entirely in his hands. If you can avoid it, don't allow someone else to persuade on your behalf. I understand that some companies won't let you speak directly with the decision maker. Instead, they want you to leave the information with an assistant who will share it with the one who makes the decision. In most cases, that assistant isn't qualified to make the presentation nor does he have the product knowledge to do so. Most times, he will present it with half the passion, half the information, and half the professionalism that you would have given. So when possible, deal with the decision-maker and give that person a clear call to action.

Two Types of Call to Action

When you are about to close a sale, presentation, or offer, it's imperative that you understand the difference between a *soft call* and a *direct call* to action. You must exercise the wisdom to know which one to use in each circumstance. If you don't ask people to do something at that moment, you might miss your only opportunity. The never-ending distractions of life will almost guarantee that you will lose it. On the other hand, if you push too hard, you might close the door for good. Nothing leaves a bitter taste in someone's mouth more than an overbearing individual. So use wisdom and discernment. A soft call to action leaves the presentation open-ended—"Think it over, and let me know if you want to move forward." A direct call to action asks for a commitment that day or with a time limit attached to it—"I can honor this offer for the next twenty-four hours."

Here are a few examples of a *soft call* to action:
- Can I have this gift wrapped for you?
- Is this something you might prefer in espresso or beige?
- Is this something you would be interested in?
- Let me know if you're interested in the acquisition.
- If you have any questions, don't hesitate to ask me.

Here are a few examples of a *direct call* to action:
- I invite you to walk over to the table where we can finalize this agreement.
- I suggest the sea bass and sautéed vegetables.
- If you're going to beat heart disease, you must exercise every day and eat sensibly.
- Cindee, will you marry me?
- If you are willing to take a step of faith, then be baptized.
- Will you agree to move forward with this order today?

Practical Steps to Become a Powerful Closer

Let me suggest some practical things you can do to become a powerful closer. First, start with a proposal you have a good chance of getting approved. Don't try and land a multimillion-dollar deal if you've never done one before. Instead, ask people with whom you have trust if you can share a few ideas with them. Only approach those you believe will say yes to your offer. It builds confidence as they agree to move forward with you. If they say no, you can ask them to give their reasons for refusing without fear of losing the relationship.

Second, visualize where you want to take your audience. Every time I speak, make a presentation, teach, or attempt to persuade, I ask myself, *What do I want my audience to do as* a result of our encounter? What do I want them to buy? What action do I want them to take? What do I want them to think? Who do I want them to follow? Sometimes, I want them to accept and remember my ideas. Other times, I want them to give money to a cause. Still other times, I want them to think beyond this life and seriously consider their plans for entering the afterlife.

Third, without spending too much money, turn on your television and watch a few infomercials. You will notice a pattern emerge in the presentations. They summarize a problem, ask an obligating question, offer a compelling solution, and give a strong call to action. You will also notice that their call to action is direct, but you don't feel overly pressured. You might be saying, "Listen, the last thing I want is to sound like an infomercial host." That's not what I am suggesting. I simply want you to grasp the way they communicate and the steps through which they take their viewers.

Fourth, acquire audio series that deal with the topic of closing. Regardless of your field, a teaching series on this topic will greatly benefit you. It will have a positive impact on your sales, legal cases, and leadership. One audio series that I highly recommend is one I mentioned earlier, Zig Ziglar's Secrets of Closing the Sale.[3] It's a twelve CD series that you can download directly from their website.

The essence of this chapter is simply this: people will give you their allegiance, money, support, or heart in exchange for something they believe is of equal or greater value. So when you give your call to action, you must first have established the need, their desire, and your solution. Once you do, you can ask them for what it is you want in exchange for your solution. If you have executed the four steps outlined in this chapter—the right summary, the right question, the right solution, and the right call to action—it will be difficult for people to walk away from your offer. Those who do will eventually realize you had the best solution and intentions for helping them.

As we bring this chapter to a close, I want to challenge you to not forget the other three sections of this book—Persuasive Leadership, Persuasive Communication, and Persuasive Solutions. The material in these sections is foundational in making you a great closer. Now, let's continue our journey in the next chapter and focus our attention on the ten most powerful closes.

Questions for discussion or personal reflection:

1. What role does an accurate summary play in becoming a powerful closer? How does a summary set the stage for the next step in the closing process?

2. What role does the right set of questions play in helping you become an effective closer? How do questions help you present the right solution?

3. How important is the right solution? How does the right solution reflect on your integrity? How important is genuineness in presenting a solution to those you aim to help?

4. Why is the call to action so important? What's the difference between a soft call and direct call to action? When should you use one instead of the other?

5. What's the most important thing you've learned in this chapter?

Chapter 8

THE TEN MOST POWERFUL CLOSES

It was one of the most convincing statements I have ever heard. I distinctly remember the words that went through my mind when I heard it: This is a guy connected to his golden thread. Brian Williams of NBC News interviewed Tim Cook, CEO of Apple, Inc., regarding the issues he faced after taking over for Steve Jobs. Tim diplomatically handled Brian's questions and at the end of the interview made a definitive statement that has stuck with me to this day. Referring to the objective of Apple he said, "Our whole role in life is to give you something you didn't know you wanted. And then once you get it, you can't imagine your life without it."[1]

That's a persuasive statement. I don't work for Apple nor have I ever received any compensation from the company. Only history can judge whether or not the organization lives up to that objective. You might ask, "What is Cook trying to sell us with such a statement?" Simply put, he sells corporate conviction. He leads people toward transformational decisions relating to the Apple brand and its products and services. Was his statement invigorating? No. Was it dynamic or polished? Not at all. It was plain and straightforward.

The most effective close is uncomplicated and without incident. When people reflect on the close they scratch their heads and say, "I really don't understand how that went so smoothly." Believe me, when you bring someone to a transformational decision, you don't want things to be turbulent and volatile. You want them to be seamless. I hope that you become so effective at closing that people will wonder how you do it.

Some experts say, "Close early, close often, but never close too late." I disagree. That's a shotgun approach to calling people to transformational decisions. Instead, I hold that the best time to close is the right time. To discover the right time, you need discernment and wisdom. Like everything else we've discussed, discernment is a skill that we develop.

Throughout this chapter, you'll discover some secrets that will give you the wisdom you need to become an effective closer. Regardless of your field, if you put into practice the things you learn in the following pages, you will become more skillful in bringing people to transformational decisions.

1. The Shutting-door Close

I told my realtor, "Here is our offer and a short list of conditions we feel must be resolved. Please tell the seller that I will honor the bid until five today. After that, we will look for a home elsewhere."

The offer was five percent under the asking price, but we made it during a time when sellers were accepting competing bids over the asking price. By noon, our realtor had not received a call. By three, there was no indication that the owner would entertain our offer. Finally, my realtor called at 4:30 p.m. and said, "The seller's realtor just called. She is meeting with the owner right now. I suggest that we wait until they have finished talking before you pull the plug." I agreed. Finally, at 5:15 p.m., our realtor called with the news, "The house is yours if you want it."

I said, "That's it? No counteroffer?"

She said, "No."

I said, "She agreed to have all the items on our list repaired at her cost?"

"Yes," she replied.

I never felt that our offer was unfair, but I was surprised that the seller responded favorably considering the high demand for housing in the area. Although I had seen the shutting-door close before, I never fully grasped the importance of using time limitation in negotiating. It became clear to me how crucial time is when we make decisions that involve the exchange of money. A limited-time offer or a closing window of opportunity gives us a sense of urgency when making transformational decisions.

You've heard the phrases before, This is a limited-time offer. Hurry while supplies last. Seating is limited. Act now, before it's too late. Who knows if you'll be hit by a truck when you walk out the door? The shutting-door approach is effective for sales representatives moving inventory, teachers motivating students to turn in their work on time, those who raise funds for time-sensitive projects, and anyone persuading people who face a potential time limit.

Whenever you present an opportunity that has a deadline, people feel prompted to take advantage of it. Whether it's an after-Christmas sale or a decision to take advantage of a last-minute cruise, urgency motivates people to take action.

If you are raising funds, communicate to your constituents the time limit for your project and when the open door will close. If you're in sales, be clear about when your special offer or sale ends. If you teach, announce that you will not be accepting any late assignments. If there is a time limitation, be straightforward about it.

Time is a precious commodity. Once we spend it, we can

never regain it. That's why when you say, "Who knows when we will see this unprecedented opportunity again?" or "Prices will never be this low again," or "Interest rates will never be this low again in our lifetime," it connects the opportunity directly to that precious commodity.

2. The Rendezvous Close

I have little to lose and much to gain, I thought. This looks like a great opportunity. The radio network had called me and said, "We'd like to put you on the air. What do you think?"

I said, "I love the idea. What's the time slot?"

"From one-thirty to two in the afternoon," the manager replied.

"Which day of the week?" I asked.

"Every day, Monday through Friday," she said.

"Excuse me," I said. "Do you mean five days a week?"

"That's correct."

Suddenly, my excitement turned into sheer intimidation. The thought of coming up with hours of radio content every week seemed daunting if not impossible. How in the world can I speak extemporaneously five days a week, 250 times a year, to over a million listeners? I asked myself.

I said, "Well, I wish I had that kind of time, but I don't. I know you are giving me the airtime and the audience is over a million actual listeners across forty different stations. But I don't have what it takes."

Three weeks passed before I received another phone call from the network manager. "Would you be willing to share the program with another host?" she asked.

"You could take three days one week and then two days the

following week. You could alternate."

After thinking about the offer, I agreed. I knew the exposure would be huge. I knew that this was an opportunity of a lifetime to reach millions of people a year. Although the commitment was big, I felt it was worth it. So I agreed. After two weeks, I had covered nearly all the material in all of my books. Somehow, though, I managed to scrounge up the material I needed for the program week after week.

Seven months passed when my co-host called to say, "My wife and I are moving to Florida. The program is all yours." My heart sank.

The owner of the three largest stations on the network called me and said, "Jason, if we can help you produce the program so that you don't have to invest more than an hour a day, would you consider being the only host? That way, the task won't seem so immense."

The price I had to pay came down to a commitment of one hour each day. The premium was the opportunity to communicate with one million people about the issues I feel most strongly about. The owner made me an offer and suggested a compromise at which we could meet. Once I clearly saw that the benefit outweighed the cost, I made the commitment. Since then, I've broadcast over 1,750 programs.

The rendezvous point in closing is a virtual place where your prospect agrees to meet you if you can provide a means to get him or her there. It says, "If I can show you how this device can save you time and money, would you be willing to purchase it?" If the prospect says yes, then you need to demonstrate the time and money it can save.

This approach is the essence of persuasion. When people see that the benefit for something outweighs what it will cost them (financially, emotionally, psychologically, spiritually, physically, or chronologically), they will make the exchange. So help them see how the benefit outweighs the cost, and they will gladly meet you at the rendezvous point.

3. The Unexpected Bonus Close

Remember Steve Harrison from the New York Publicity Summit? He once said to me, "Sell people what they want, and give them what they need."

I said, "Steve, shouldn't we sell people what they need?"

He said, "No. People buy what they want. They may or may not buy what they need. So give them what they need when you can."

His thoughts were spot on. How many of us buy what we truly need? How many of us run three miles a day? How many people faithfully attend church, visit the doctor once a year, brush and floss between meals, and get eight hours of sleep? People reluctantly go to the doctor. They reluctantly eat their vegetables. They reluctantly buy gasoline. No one gets excited about these things, but we need them.

When you deliver a presentation, make a sale, settle a case out of court, or look for people to buy into your ideas, offer them what they want. Then give them what they need as a bonus. Giving people what they need solves a problem that they may wrestle with in the back of their minds.

This approach offers an unexpected benefit during the close that makes it difficult to resist. You've probably heard the phrase *But wait, there's more!* Or, *If you act now, we'll include this additional item as an added bonus*. You can call it "sweetening the pot," an "added incentive," or simply an "enticement." The end result is the same. As you aim to lead people to transformational decisions, you offer them something unanticipated that highly benefits them.

Toward the end of Steve Jobs' keynote speeches announcing new Apple products, he would say, "There's one more thing." It was an added bonus to which people had difficulty responding, "I am not interested." That was the phrase he used when introducing the iMac, wireless laptops, displays, iPods, Apple TV, iTunes Music Store, and desktop computers. Whether or not you are a fan of Apple, it's hard to refute that Apple grew from $5 billion in revenue in the 1980s to become the largest company in the world in 2013 according to the Financial Times.[2]

When you are hiring someone or simply applying for a position, if you think there is something you can do that will tip the scales in your favor, reveal your unexpected bonus as the negotiation is about to end. This might include statements like "I might also mention that I am bilingual." Or, "If you make a commitment to move forward today, I will include delivery at no charge."

Some businesses or representatives never negotiate, nor do they give an unexpected bonus. They feel that doing so diminishes the value of their product, service, or idea. However, the average customer in any marketplace wants one thing—a good deal. I have yet to meet someone who didn't. So under promise and over deliver. Give them more than what they expect and they will buy from you again, hire you as a consultant, or sign up for your next course.

4. The No-nonsense Close

As I mentioned in chapter 2, a number of years ago I came to one of the most important life-changing crossroads of my life. I had to lose over sixty pounds. Not only was I out of shape and miserable, but my blood pressure and cholesterol were much too high for my age. My doctor assured me that I wouldn't be around to see any grandchildren if I didn't alter my course. Talk about a persuasive close.

I remember two slogans that particularly motivated me. The first was "Just Do It." It was an unambiguous and sharp reminder that I had no excuses. The second was a sign that read, "When is the best time to get in shape?" Truthfully, the answer was and is now. If I say in a month, I am not being honest with myself. The best time to take care of my body is today.

This second phrase points to a close that is one of the most basic yet effective. You can apply this principle to nearly every field. I call it the no-nonsense close. It states the obvious. It's factual and practical. This is how it works. Once you've established the validity of your idea, product, or service, you ask three simple questions.

The first question is *Can you see how this diet will help you get in shape?* Once your prospect agrees, you ask the second question, *Are you interested in getting in shape?* If they answer positively, then the closing question is *If you were going to start getting in shape, when would be the best time to start?* This is an effective way to help people move beyond procrastination.

This approach works especially well when presenting a product or an idea that saves time or money. In the first question simply change the word *diet* to whatever product or idea you offer. Also, change the words *get in shape* to *save money* (or *time*). In the second and third questions, change *getting into shape* to *saving money* (or *time*). If your prospect is honest, in most cases the answer is *now*. They will experience the same feeling that came over me when I read the sign *When is the best time to get in shape?* I knew there is no better time than now to get healthy.

When faced with the truth, people do not like to think that they are neglecting something beneficial for their company, family, or themselves. If they do not move forward with your suggestion, most likely there is a hidden objection that you have not discovered. You can discover that objection by asking what reason(s) prevents them from moving forward with your offer.

5. The Visualization Close

The speaker said it only once, but I caught his subtle prediction. "Today, more than half of you will sign up for this program." The presentation was good but not great. In forty-five minutes, he talked about how he turned his life around from being overweight, sick, and in debt. The most important thing he did, though, was to suggest to his audience a scenario where they benefit from his system.

"Imagine walking into a store and buying anything off the rack," he said. "Imagine having the money to buy the things you want to buy when you want to buy them. I have no doubt if you use my system, that's the life you'll have within twenty-four months."

I know that everyone wants to be thin and healthy and have money in the bank. But still, on a scale of 1 to 10, I would have given his presentation a 7. I didn't think he was compelling enough to motivate half the audience to shell out $495 for a workbook and audio series. Boy, was I wrong.

When he was finished, nearly seventy percent of the 150 people in attendance walked to the five tables set up against the back wall and either wrote a check or handed his assistant a credit card. That's over fifty thousand dollars. I thought to myself, I must have missed something. Then I started to break down his presentation. I realized that he successfully helped people visualize themselves experiencing the benefits of his system. More importantly, they experienced a feeling that came as a result of that visualization.

Once people envision themselves experiencing the benefits of a product or service, it's easy for them to take ownership of it. As long as the call to action isn't complicated, they will follow the steps to get what they want.

Statements like, "Imagine moving into retirement without any fear of lowering your standard of living." Or, "Imagine the peace of mind knowing that your wife and children are in a vehicle that has the best maintenance record on the road." And, "Do you long to be happy, healthy, and reasonably prosperous? Well, that's exactly what this plan aims to help you attain."

Let me underscore the importance of being someone of integrity. Remember, disingenuous persuasion is manipulation. Only present something if you are convinced it is the best solution for those you aim to serve. Be sincere. Be honest. Yes, help your prospects envision adopting your plan or product, but only if it is truly beneficial.

Whether you raise funds, speak in churches, sell products or services, or motivate high school students to prepare for college, the visualization approach helps people see themselves in a better place in the future and makes their call to action much easier.

6. The Sherlock Holmes Close

Recently I sat down with the board of directors of one of the largest churches in America. They were going through a difficult transition. Their founding pastor was now advanced in years. Their income was declining and the once-solid donor base was dying off. Because of that, they were on the verge of bankruptcy.

"Jason, what is your advice for us?" they asked.

"It sounds like you need to rediscover your purpose," I said, "Tell me, why do you exist?"

"The church exists for the television program," they replied.

Somewhat puzzled by their answer, I kept my poker face and asked the next question: "Why does the television program exist?"

For a few minutes they looked at each other and uttered a phrase or two that hardly seemed connected to the question.

I continued, "It looks like you forgot your mission. All the problems you're facing caused your vision to become clouded."

"Don't you exist to help people with a message of hope?" I asked.

"Yes! That's what our mission is, helping people with a message of hope," one of the directors blurted out.

"You probably don't want to hear this," I said, "but if you want to turn this $25 million organization around, this entity needs one focus, one mission, and one person to lead it."

"But we want something different. We want team leadership. That's what all the business books are talking about," one of the members added.

"A football team has an owner, a head coach, and a general manager," I replied, "but when the ball is snapped, everything always comes down to a quarterback who decides what to do with the ball. In your case, you don't want a different person speaking each Sunday, especially when the congregants have had one dynamic speaker for the past thirty-five years."

"But what about those business models that champion team leadership?" the member asked.

"How many of those authors have real-world experience in churches?" I asked. "Is there one model that has worked in a church or non-profit organization with a $25 million budget?" The director was silent.

I continued, "You have called some of the greatest communicators in America to come and help fill your pulpit, but that is not what you need. None of them demonstrated the ability to grasp your vision, nor did they demonstrate the wherewithal to commandeer this ship. Instead of going outside of the organization, look for someone within your church who you trust, who understands the vision, and who has the commitment to see you through. When you have eliminated all other candidates, then the one that is left, no matter how unlikely, is the one you need to entrust with leading the organization."

The founder, along with everyone else in the boardroom, looked over at one person, the founder's son. He was committed to the vision but was always overlooked. He was educated but never given a chance. People loved him but because of his father's charisma, he had difficulty standing out on his own.

Sometimes the best solution is the most obvious. Sometimes the most obvious is right under our noses, but because of all the competing ideas, we are unable to see it. That's why we need to help people see what might be obvious to us but invisible to them. If we aim to lead people to transformational decisions, we need to help them eliminate the impossible so that they can see the best remaining option.

Why do I call this the Sherlock Holmes close? Mr. Holmes said on more than one occasion, "When you have eliminated the impossible, whatever remains, however improbable, must be the truth." This is nothing less than the best solution by process of elimination. Sometimes people have difficulty seeing the clear-cut choice. In their mind, certain things are impossible, improbable, or not worth entertaining. Paradigms become clouded with competing ideas and emotions. The Sherlock Holmes approach is a close that helps prospects become open to possibilities and sheds light on the situation.

So when using this close, you can say, "Here is another option we might want to consider." Or perhaps you might say, "It seems as though our options are narrowed to one or two." Whether you are working on a court case, making a crucial point in a debate, or challenging students to think outside the box, the Sherlock Holmes close (elimination of the impossible) works well to lead people toward a decision they would otherwise never consider.

7. The Indisputable-truth Close

"Fifty thousand dollars for paper and ink," the purchasing agent whined. "You've got to be kidding me." That was his reaction when I showed him the quote for the payroll checks. The company was a major manufacturer in my territory. They always asked three competitors to make offers. Our price was thirty percent higher than what he paid one of our competitors the year before. "How do you justify the cost?" he asked.

I looked him in the eye with complete sincerity and said, "I know that our price is higher. Let me tell you why. Quality is our reputation. It's our number one asset. It's our priority. In all the years I've worked for this organization, I have never once heard a customer complain about poor quality. With your permission, I would like to ask you a question."

He nodded.

I asked, "How much did the previous mishap with your payroll checks cost you in terms of downtime, employee headaches, reprinting, and damage to your printer?" He sat in silence. "You don't have to answer that," I said. "My guess is that it cost you much more than the number written on the quote in front of you. I am fully confident that our payroll checks will work perfectly with your software and printers, and if they don't, we will cover the cost to replace them and repair any damage they cause to your system."

Then I made a statement based upon something that could not be refuted. "I would much rather sit here and justify the higher price and confidently share with you our commitment to quality so that you can have peace of mind, than apologize for poor quality and unprecedented incompetence like our competitor has to do. Wouldn't you agree?"

The purchasing agent approved the price quote and issued a purchase order. Four weeks later, I received a phone call. "We'll see just how committed you are to quality," said the voice on the other end of the phone. It was the purchasing agent.

"What do you mean," I asked.

"We received the checks," he said. "They are the wrong color!"

That was not what I wanted to hear. "Do the checks work in your printer?" I asked.

"Yes."

"Even though they are the wrong color, can you use them

until we can replace them?" I asked.

"Yes."

I said, "I think I have a solution that will work in your favor. Keep the first 2,500 checks and use them. In the meantime, I will contact our factory and have them reprint the checks in the right color starting with the check number that continues after the 2,500 that we are giving you. I want you to know that your business is important to us, and we are committed to your satisfaction."

After looking into what happened, we discovered that in fact the customer wrote down the incorrect color number. Our factory printed what they were told to print, but the customer wasn't satisfied. Later, when I showed him the color he originally specified, he acknowledged his mistake and apologized. He said, "You know, I see why your price is higher than your competitors, and I appreciate your commitment to quality."

The indisputable-truth close is powerful. The statement wouldn't you agree that, followed by an indisputable truth establishes the true priority when we aim to persuade others. Other examples include, "Wouldn't you agree that knowing your family will not lose your home is worth the investment for life insurance?" Or, "Wouldn't you agree that it's better to pay a little more than what you expected than less than you should?"[2] One of my favorites that I learned from Zig Ziglar is "It's easier to explain price just once than apologize for poor quality or service for a lifetime."[3]

8. The People-before-you Close

He was one of the best fundraisers I'd ever met. He had a keen ability to make everyone feel that they were contributing

The Ten Most Powerful Closes

to the most important project in the world. There were about 250 people sitting in the banquet hall. We had just finished a nice dinner when he began his compelling story. He wrapped up his remarks by saying, "Many years ago, pioneers came across the United States and took arrows in the back. In the midst of an unforgiving and rough world, they forged a new way of life. Today, you and I enjoy a better life because people went before us and paved the way."

Then he said, "Nearly half of all men and one third of all women will be directly affected by cancer in their lifetime. In the same way pioneers went before us, I am asking you to pave the way for those whose lives you can make better. Your gift today can save a life tomorrow. Pioneers knew that you and I would follow in their footsteps. You know that others will follow us. Let's work together to eliminate the deadly effects of cancer. Please make your generous contribution to . . . ," then he named the organization.

There was a noticeable change in the atmosphere in the banquet hall. The servers stopped serving. People whose loved ones had struggled with cancer wiped tears from their eyes. You couldn't hear the clang of a single plate or glass. Instead, people ripped checks from their checkbooks. There was an overwhelming sense that we were participating in one of the most meaningful missions of society—giving time and money to help save lives.

Asking people to give money in exchange for a feeling is always a challenge. When people give to a charitable work, they don't have the euphoria of putting the big screen TV in the back of their SUV or seeing the look on their children's faces when they give them the newest video game console. What they receive from their charitable gift is a feeling—of helping, of fulfillment.

Fundraising is not easy, but it can be rewarding. The people-before-you approach is effective when raising money for non-profit organizations. It's a powerful close that shows continuity.

If you are raising capital for a start-up company, this approach also can be effective. Anytime you ask people to invest their capital in a business venture, they will want two primary things: a good return on investment and their money back as soon as possible. As long as these two requirements are met, people will prefer to invest their funds in a project they feel is going to make a difference and that sheds a positive light on them. As you illustrate the manner in which predecessors invested, it's important that you show how those investments impacted lives to the present day. Then encourage your benefactors to finance your endeavor because present-day investors will continue to make a great impact on future generations.

If you raise funds for a new church building, for example, you can say, "Years ago, people gave money so that we could have a place to meet. They gave believing that you and I would come to this place and worship. And they were right. You and I are here. Now I want to ask you to give to _____ (name of new project) believing that future generations will come and experience transformation as well."

We love to be a part of a continuous process that makes a difference. When we feel connected to a great opportunity, venture, or mission, we gladly give our time and money to help advance that cause. Give people the ability to see how they can be part of something historical and meaningful, and they will make transformational decisions.

9. The Test-drive Close

As soon as I put on the suit, walked out of the dressing room, and saw my wife's face, I knew I was in trouble. I tried everything I could think of to sabotage the purchase. It was more money than I wanted to spend. I was shopping in a store I had no business shopping in. Truthfully, the suit was beautiful. I had never seen such a wonderful cut. But did I mention the price was more than I wanted to pay?

The young professional assistant named Yoshie walked over and chimed in, "What a fantastic suit." Obviously, she wasn't helping my cause. I grinned ever so slightly and returned to the dressing room.

When I came out, Yoshie asked me, "Well, what do you think?"

I said, "It's gorgeous. Yoshie, you're a very good sales representative, but I need to talk this over with my wife."

Yoshie said, "No problem. Take all the time you need." She knew that the longer that suit was on my body, the more likely I was to buy it. She withdrew about twenty feet away, giving me the privacy I requested.

Turning to Cindee, I said in a low voice, "I don't think I'll feel confortable owning this suit."

With a puzzled look on her face my wife asked, "What do you mean? You speak at large conventions. You have television appearances. You make important presentations. I know it's not cheap, but I think for what you do, you need a suit like this."

"I don't know, sweetheart," I said.

"Tell you what," Cindee responded. "Slip the suit jacket on one more time and have a look at it."

I returned to the dressing room and put the jacket on for

a second time. I was growing accustomed to all the positive reinforcement. When I looked in the mirror, I began to see myself the way my wife and the others in the store saw me. More importantly, I began to feel something. With that feeling came a sense of ownership.

Then my wife said, "Sweetheart, I think you should get the suit, but if you don't want it, we can go somewhere else and find you a cheap suit." With that, Yoshie returned and said, "How do you feel in that gorgeous suit?"

Guess what happened next? I bought the suit.

Have you ever seen a child playing with a toy in a toy store, and the mom says, "Time to go. Let's put the toy down." If the child has played with the toy longer than five minutes, usually he orchestrates a strong protest or in some cases a conniption. Nobody wants to be the bad guy, especially a parent who has to rip a toy out of his child's hands and give it back to the clerk. It's not a pretty sight. Why is that? Once a child has the toy for a period of time, he takes ownership of it. He becomes emotionally attached to it.

One of the best closes is the test-drive close. That is precisely the reason car dealerships allow people to drive a vehicle before making the purchase. The same is true for most clothing stores.

According to the NY Daily News, close to fifty percent of every article of clothing sold online is returned. However, only thirty percent of clothes purchased in a retail store is returned. What's the difference? People experience an in-store test drive. So why do companies allow people to test-drive clothing? Buyers are more likely to walk out of a store with the garment they want. That means that millions of dollars are spent in these stores because people have the freedom to try the product before they spend the money. Further, a return policy gives people added peace of mind that they can change their minds later.[4]

The test-drive approach also gives people peace of mind. The bridge isn't burned when they walk out the door. Many electronic devices, kitchen appliances, and certain domestic hardware come with a return policy that is called buyer's remorse. This is nothing less than a two-week or one month test-drive close, depending on the manufacturer.

If you can offer your customers, clients, or prospects a window of opportunity in which they can embrace what you offer, they will be much more likely to take ownership of it and appreciate their acquisition. In most cases, they will keep it for the duration of its usefulness.

10. The Past-precedent Close

I asked the front desk clerk, "Your name tag has the city you're from written under your name. Tell me, what made you move from Lansing, Michigan, to Las Vegas?"

"Three hundred ten," he said.

"Three hundred ten what?" I asked.

"Three hundred ten days of sunshine." He looked down for a moment to continue checking us into our hotel room, then he continued, "You see, where I come from there are 180 days of gray sky."

I never thought about it that way. As a native Californian, we have more than our fair share of sunny skies (and drought), and it would never occur to me to move somewhere just because the weather was more moderate. Still, Las Vegas' 310 days of sunshine beat Southern California weather hands down. There is something to be said about a climate that is so consistent.

Las Vegas is famous for many things, some are admirable,

others are not so admirable. Since its incorporation in 1911, it has grown exponentially. The reason is it has a strong precedent that hardly changes. The weather spawned a massive surge in construction of hotels with huge buffets. Gambling was legalized in 1931 and the construction of Hoover Dam finished in 1935. This gave way to continued expansion and growth. The consistency in the weather is what gave Las Vegas its foundation. This is one of the reasons people choose to vacation there and why companies hold their conferences there. Why else would people fly in from all over the world to vacation in the middle of the desert? After all, if you absolutely had to be in a place where the weather is hot, dry, sunny, and had a plethora of activities, which city would you think of? A strong consistent precedent is the foundation for a powerful close that says, "Some things never change." This close is all about track record.

Let's take a look at the following phrases: That's the way we've always done it. If it's not broke, don't fix it. Why break precedent? That's what has worked in the past. Let's go with what works.

When lawyers try a case, for example, they use the past-precedent approach nearly every time. They research every possible court case and decision that is similar in circumstances. Then when they find several strong similarities, they present that to the court as evidence so that the judge or jury will decide in their favor. When a judge and jury see a precedent, they sense the weight of making a decision that is congruent with those previous decisions.

The past-precedent close works well in debate, business, law, teaching, and just about any area where you aim to persuade people. If you are selling services, you can use a statement like "For nearly seventy-five years, families have come to us to solve their irrigation problems." Or, "Based upon your purchasing history with us, you seem to order ten pounds of dark chocolate each holiday season. Would you like to continue your tradition?" And, "I completely understand your interest in doing something creative, but breaking precedent could put your deadline at risk."

Every one of the closes mentioned in this chapter is unique, but they all have one thing in common. They must be contextualized to fit your needs and field of expertise. Please don't repeat the example sentences verbatim. Instead, look at their intent and then change the wording to fit your specific needs.

Study some of the persuasive people you know. Ask yourself what makes them so compelling. Why do people follow their advice? What makes them attractive leaders? Odds are, they know how to close effectively, and with that skill comes impressive results.

Throughout this chapter, we've looked at ten powerful closes. First, with the shutting-door close, we learned that when people sense that there is a time limit placed upon their opportunity, it can create urgency and a desire to decide in favor of what you recommend. The second close is a technique that seeks common ground or a virtual meeting place, providing you can show your prospect that it will be beneficial. I call it the rendezvous close. The third close aims to tip the scales in your favor by adding an unexpected bonus to the agreement.

A no-nonsense approach is the fourth close. It states what is obvious, factual, and practical. After establishing the validity of your product or idea, you can ask three simple questions to close. The fifth close uses visualization to help people see themselves experiencing the benefits of a product or service. As they do, it's easy for them to take ownership. The Sherlock Holmes close eliminates the impossible so that those you aim to serve can see the best remaining option. This close helps eliminate confusion when there are many competing ideas.

The seventh close is the indisputable-truth approach. When you share an indisputable truth and how it is connected to a true priority, it is a powerful approach to persuading others. Next is the people-before-you close that points to the way that past generations have laid a foundation for the life, practices, and direction we have today. It encourages people to build on the foundations of those who have gone before us.

The test-drive close is the ninth approach, and it encourages people to try a product or idea. Once they do, they have a greater tendency to take ownership. Finally, the past-precedent close looks at unwavering patterns that people can depend on when making transformational decisions. When there is no room for error, people will pay more, and go out of their way for the peace of mind that this close brings.

Become familiar with these closes and adapt them to your situation. Add other closes to your repertoire as you feel confident, and soon you will be highly effective in the skill of closing. Through it all, search for the best way to solve the problems of those you aim to serve. As you do, you will become highly effective at closing a transaction.

Questions for discussion or personal reflection:

1. Of all the closes we've studied, which one stands out the most to you? Why does it stand out? Is there one close that you feel is most applicable to your area of expertise?

2. What are some examples you can give of the shutting-door close in your area or field of expertise? In what ways does it prompt people to action?

3. Why is the rendezvous close the essence of persuasion?

4. Why is past precedent so important as it relates to guarantees and warrantees?

5. What's the most important thing you've learned in this chapter?

Conclusion

At the end of one of our conferences, a 6 foot 3 inch man weighing over 240 pounds approached me at the base of the stage. He was taller, more muscular, and probably fifteen years younger than me. With a stern look he said, "In your keynote speech, you said that parents are foolish if they don't get their spiritual lives in order and find a healthy church. Are you saying that I am a fool?" Standing in front of him were two little girls, one five, the other three. I asked him if they were his. He said yes. I gestured toward them and said, "Do you want these precious little girls to grow up and fall into the hands of human trafficking or become addicted to drugs?" No, he said.

I said, "Do you want them to marry abusive husbands?" Again, he said no. I continued, "Do you want them to live a life of delinquency or become victims?" He said no. Then I asked, "Tell me, who is going to be their role model for living an ethical and morally grounded life? Who's going to set the standard for them? If you don't, who will? Be a man! Be a good father and be the spiritual example you should, and get your spiritual life in order."

He lowered his head and simply nodded. He was persuaded. Looking down at his daughters, he knew he needed to become a better man. Not only did he need to get his spiritual life in order (for his sake), but his wife and kids needed him to be a better husband and dad as well. Tom made a transformational decision at that moment that will forever alter his life course and the generations that follow him.

Those who have the power to persuade are first and foremost persuaded. They have already bought into the idea, product, direction, or plan they present. Their enthusiasm is an extension

Conclusion

of their conviction that says, "I know the way. I know this is the right choice. I believe beyond any doubt that this is the right course of action." Their conviction is based upon integrity and honesty.

Throughout this book, we talked about some transformational concepts. We discovered in the first section how integrity is perhaps the most important characteristic of someone people want to follow. Without integrity, there is no trust. Without trust, there is no relationship. Without a relationship, no one is persuaded, nor do they follow. All great leaders display dedication, wisdom, honor, and encouragement. Above all, they know their calling and how to help those they lead feel connected to their own golden thread.

Next, we looked at the importance of having a clear and healthy perception (paradigm) and what we can do to develop one. Only when we see our own path clearly can we have a vision of the future and lead others toward their promised land. As long as we are connected to our golden thread, we can lead with conviction, enhance our sense of timing, and establish an effective plan.

The second section dealt with the importance of becoming a great communicator. Leadership is important, but if we cannot communicate effectively, then we have little hope of leading people to transformational decisions. The starting point for great communicators is a healthy internal dialogue. The conversation we have with ourselves is the most important one we will ever have. We also learned that persuasion is nothing more than a transference of feeling. When we clearly transfer the way we feel about what we present, sell, or hold to be true, people become persuaded. Great communicators have a keen ability to get to the point effectively and utilize the powerful tool of storytelling.

Effective communicators develop special skills in order to reach their audiences. They display the ability to see their prospect's need and desire and understand the difference between the two. They can read their audience and make adjustments quickly and smoothly. They are not only gifted in narrative communication, but they also share stories about one main character with whom the audience can identify.

In the third section, we looked at the importance of being effective problem solvers and not being intimidated by the glass ceiling or barrier that keeps us from moving forward. Whenever we face an objection, we must first reconnect with our greatest asset and ensure that we use our leverage to overcome it. This sets the stage for us to learn the four important steps to become first-rate negotiators so that we know the best approach when the answer seems to be a definite no.

We learned the five basic objections to every potential transaction. Many times people lack the need, money, urgency, desire, or trust to make a decision. However with time, circumstances and people change. Nothing is set in concrete and what might be considered a luxury one day becomes a necessity the next week.

In the fourth section, we learned how to master the skill of great closing. There are four steps that great closers use to lead people to transformational decisions. They are articulating the right summary; asking the right question; providing the right solution; and giving the right call to action.

Finally, we concluded the section with ten powerful closes. We also learned the ways, fields of expertise, and applications in which they can be useful. There we found helpful insights to becoming an effective closer no matter what your occupation.

Conclusion

Before we conclude our journey together, let me leave you with perhaps one of the most important things I can share. In the introduction of this book, I mentioned that I came from a crazy family. I also mentioned I would share with you how I managed to overcome some of the debilitating and dysfunctional craziness in my home in order to become the person I am today. What I am about to share with you is the essence of reaching your greatest potential. If you are going to become someone who persuasively leads, communicates, solves, and closes, you must grow equally in each of the following areas.

The first and most important area is spiritual. Every great leader I know is in the process of knowing God and developing his or her relationship with Him. Why is this so important? For starters, we'll be dead much longer than alive so we need to be prepared for this life and the next. Spiritual growth means that we follow God's leadership in every area of our life, and that has the most significant impact of anything we can do. It will impact your integrity, character, paradigm, wisdom, direction, outlook, and faith for the future. It impacts your relationships, marriage, children, and the way you interact with society. As I said to the young man after the conference, get your spiritual life in order if you haven't already begun to do so. Faith in Christ helped me overcome the craziness and dysfunction that kept our family from moving forward for many generations.

Second, taking care of yourself physically is imperative. You can't get to the top of the mountain if you don't have the gas to get there. Your body is your vehicle, and you must maintain it. Give yourself healthy fuel, enough exercise, and plenty of sleep. Only after I lost sixty pounds did I begin to have the clarity of mind and mental stamina to handle the challenges of life.

Third, your financial well-being is essential for the emotional, physical, and psychological security of your household. Few things wear on you like debt, lack of funds, or fear of losing what you have. Find a financial plan such as Financial Peace University (www.daveramsey.com) or some other highly recommended educational program to help build this important area of your life.

Fourth, aim to have healthy friendships and family relationships. Surround yourself with people who pick you up instead of tear you down. Many times we are attracted to people or become involved romantically with someone based upon chemistry. We like the way we feel when we are around them. This can be good, but it can also be detrimental if the relationship does not help us become a better person. So choose your friends and your relationships wisely. If they don't have your best interest in mind, develop relationships with those who will help you develop emotionally and spiritually.

Fifth, continue your education in order to maintain mental vitality. Mental vitality keeps you sharp and helps you in every one of the areas mentioned above. Listen to audio teaching series while you're on the road. Subscribe to blogs. Take university classes. Read educational books. Don't let your greatest asset waste away by constantly watching television. The mentally sharp person is much more effective at the skill of persuasion.

Finally, continue to look for ways to excel in your career. Learn from those who have gone before you. Study the experts in your field. Find a mentor who can selflessly guide you to the next level. Then, look for ways to mentor others. Don't ever think for one moment that you've arrived or have reached your greatest potential. Don't ever think that it's beneath you to help or serve others. Remember, arrogance is like bad breath—

CONCLUSION

everyone knows you have it except you.

Each of these six areas is so important. Continuing to grow will keep balance in your life and allow you to become someone who is highly persuasive.

I trust that this book has been insightful and helpful to you. My desire is that you experience great breakthroughs as you utilize the power to persuade!

Endnotes

Chapter 1
1. (http://www.upi.com/Odd_News/2013/11/15/New-Hampshire-cab-driver-nearing-90th-birthday/UPI-96951384562571/)
2. Zig Ziglar, Zig Ziglar's Little Book of Big Quotes (Plano, TX: Ziglar, Inc., 2008).
3. http://www.forbes.com/sites/louisefron/2013/06/24/six-reasons-your-best-employees-quit-you/

Chapter 2
1. https://itunes.apple.com/app/itunes-u/id490217893?mt=8&ls=1)
2. Zig Ziglar, Secrets of Closing the Sale audio series, www.ziglar.com

Chapter 3
1. http://www.ziglar.com/motivation/encouraging-yourself-brings-about-change

Chapter 5
1. Nido Qubein, https://www.youtube.comwatch?v=BaTX0t_3Psg
2. http://www.ziglar.com/speakers/jason-frennziglar-motivational-speaker

Chapter 6
1. Zig Ziglar, Secrets of Closing the Sale audio series

Endnotes

Chapter 7

1. Zig Ziglar, Secrets of Closing the Sale audio series, disk 5, track 5
2. http://www.k-state.edu/media/newsreleases/jul13/predictingdivorce71113.html
3. http://www.ziglar.com/store/type/downloads

Chapter 8

1. http://articles.latimes.com/2012/dec/06/business/la-fi-tn-transcript-apple-ceo-tim-cook-interviewed-on-nbc-20121206/4
2. http://im.ft-static.com/content/images/67c810a4-ae5b-11e2-bdfd-00144feabdc0.pdf
3. Zig Ziglar, Secrets of Closing the Sale audio series
4. http://www.nydailynews.com/life-style/fashion/online-retailers-size-shoppers-cut-returns-article-1.1469499

Acknowledgements

Thank you, Don and Maxine Judkins, for twenty-five years of friendship, support, and partnership. You are some of the finest people Cindee and I know. Much of what I have written in the pages of this book has come from the servanthood influence and example you have been to us!

Thank you, Rick Cortez, for never saying no to my request for help! You are a generous friend and an incredibly gifted young man. Thank you for designing the cover and for sharing your creative business insights with me!

Thank you, Kathleen Stephens, for editing this book. Your professionalism has helped hundreds of thousands of people become more effective and persuasive as they are touched by your literary influence. You are a blessing to work with!

Thank you, Chanel Frenn, for being the first set of eyes for this document. You helped bring clarity and relevance to this book. I am proud of you and stand in admiration of all you are becoming!

Thank you, Signature Equipovision, for all you do to help people overcome the obstacles that hold them back. Juan and Alicia Ruelas, Borden Newman, Claudio Moreno, Olidia Mejorado, Luis Juarez, and every other member of that great organization, you are making a significant difference in the lives of tens of thousands of people every month!

Thank you to all my friends at the Ziglar Corporation for your outstanding example of integrity, humility, and professionalism. Laurie Magers, Margarett Garrett, Bryan Flanagan, Michael McGowan, Julie Norman, Jill Tibbels, Kayla Mitchell, and Tom Ziglar, you are all some of the finest in sales training!

Notes

Power To Persuade

Notes

Power To Persuade

Notes

Power To Persuade